FOOTPATH WALKS
IN AND AROUND
THE PEAK DISTRICT NATIONAL PARK

by
Pat and Peter Tidsall

FOLLOW THE COUNTRY CODE

Guard against all risk of fire
Fasten all gates
Keep dogs under proper control
Keep to paths across farmland
Avoid damaging fences, hedges and walls
Leave no litter
Safeguard water supplies
Protect wildlife, wild plants and trees
Go carefully on country roads
Respect the life of the countryside

---

18 circular footpath walks of 6 to 8 miles

The route maps are based upon the Ordnance Survey mapping with the permission of The Controller of Her Majesty's Stationery Office © Crown Copyright 399531.

Printed in Great Britain

ISBN 0 85100 13⁣ and Peter Tidsall 2002

DI⁣ ⁣TED
Heri⁣ ⁣1 3HE
T⁣ ⁣688

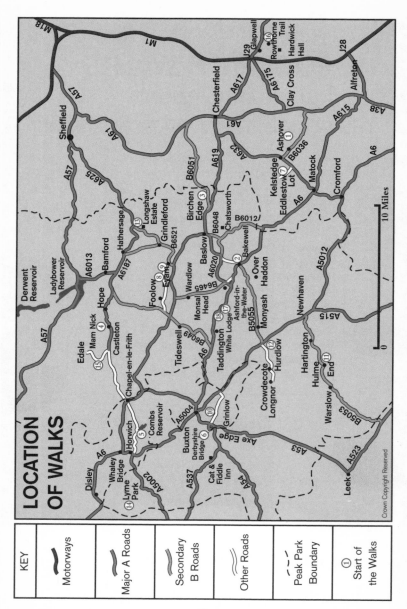

LOCATION OF WALKS

KEY

～～	Motorways
━━	Major A Roads
━	Secondary B Roads
～～	Other Roads
- - -	Peak Park Boundary
①	Start of the Walks

Crown Copyright Reserved

10 Miles

0

2

INDEX OF WALKS

INDEX OF WALKS

KEY TO SYMBOLS USED ON THE ROUTE MAPS

`~ ᴗ ⌐`	Route of Walk	`∿`	Rivers
	Main A Roads		Woods
	Secondary Roads	✝	Church with Spire
	Roads over 4m	✝	Church with Tower
	Roads under 4m	**P**	Car Park
	Other Roads, Drives or Tracks	**C**	Craft Centre
	Trails	**P.H.**	Public House
	Railways (Main Line)	**H**	Hotel
	Railways (Mineral Line)	**T.R.**	Tearoom
		R	Restaurant

INTRODUCTION

Although the Peak National Park, as well as being the first to be established, is accepted as one of the most beautiful and popular walking and rambling areas in the country, there are equally interesting walks bordering the Park. We have included four of them in this book.

Taking into account the books already published with the same format, which we have continued to use in this book, it seemed logical and helpful to fill a gap between the red book *Circular Walks in the Peak Park* and the green book *Short Walks in the Peak Park* on the one hand and the somewhat longer walks of 6 to 12 miles in the blue book *Walks in the Peak National Park*.

Therefore in this turquoise book *Footpath Walks in and around the Peak National Park* we present 18 walks of 6-8 miles.

All the walks are along statutory footpaths and bridleways. It is advisable to wear stout footwear, ideally boots and thick woollen socks, in view of the rocky and sometimes muddy terrain. The weather in North Derbyshire can be very unpredictable and warm waterproof clothing should be part of your equipment. It can be substantially colder at the higher parts of a walk. A sketch map is provided for every walk but the O.S. 1:25000 scale maps of The Peak District will also be very useful and informative. The Touring Map 4 *Peak District* gives some interesting information and is useful in interpreting the directions given in each walk

Please note that the route instructions, after crossing stiles or going through gates, are given as if you stand with your back to the stile you have just crossed. The details given were accurate at the time of walking. It seems however that in the Peak Park area a number of stiles are being replaced with gates.

We hope that you will derive as much enjoyment and recreation from the use of this book as we have done in putting it together.

Pat and Peter Tidsall

KELSTEDGE – SPITEWINTER

Ashover – Kelstedge – Uppertown – Alicehead – Spitewinter – Press Reservoirs – Northedge – Ashover

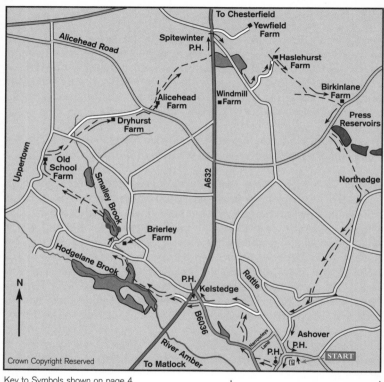

Key to Symbols shown on page 4

0   1 Mile

MAP: O.S. Explorer 269 Chesterfield and Alfreton.

PARKING: Grid Ref. SK350632.

DIRECTIONS: From Matlock town centre at the Crown island, take the A615 Alfreton road and Chesterfield road A632. In about ½ mile turn left to follow the A632 Chesterfield road. After 3½ miles in Kelstedge, turn right by *The Kelstedge Inn* to follow the B6036 to Ashover. In about ½ mile and just before entering the village, turn left signed Rattle. Drive along Narrowleys Lane and at the T-junction turn right into Ashover. Take the second left turn by *The Black Swan*. Turn right into the small car park by the tennis courts.

WALK DESCRIPTION:

Domesday Book recorded a village beyond the ash forest, with 14 smallholders, a church, a priest and an inn. The villagers made shoes, baskets, lace and nails. Nearby Rattle, so called because the machines rattled so much, was a stocking-making village. The Amber Valley below Ashover has been called ' the valley of silence and wild flowers'. This walk is certainly a very peaceful one and follows undulating paths and tracks away from the more populated areas of the Peak Park. There are a number of refreshment stops in Ashover, Kelstedge and *The Three Horseshoes* in Spitewinter.

ROUTE INSTRUCTIONS:

1. Leave the car park and turn left down the road. At *The Black Swan* turn left to follow the sign Stretton 3 ¾. Pass the church on your right. Turn right below the church to follow a driveway, at the end of which keep straight on along a grass track, first with the churchyard then a playing field on your right and crossing one stile.
2. Turn right along the road passing the turn to Rattle. Just before the converted chapel cross the squeeze stile on your right.
3. Walk past the 'Chapel' on your left and just before the field corner turn left under a sycamore tree. Cross the field diagonally. Go through a stile in the field corner. Turn right up the next field to cross a stile in the field corner.
4. Turn left along the lane and at the first bend follow the Footpath sign. Continue past 'Marsh Green' to follow a track up to the road.
5. Turn right up the road for about 75 metres then turn left down The Causeway, passing *The Kelstedge Inn*. Cross the A632 to walk up Vernon Lane.
6. At the end of the lane keep straight on following a narrow enclosed path which shortly widens out through the wood. Follow the woodland path down across a stone footbridge to go through a small metal gate ahead.
7. Follow the path which climbs the hill then meanders along the undulating valley side to a gate. Go over the stile onto the road.
8. Turn left to follow the road for about 175 metres then the first turn right

along another minor road for about 175 metres. Just after a left-hand bend and opposite Brierley Farm, turn left.

9. Walk up a few metres of a driveway then turn right through a waymarked metal gate. Bear left past standing stones to go through an old kissing gate then on up wall steps.

10. Follow the path passing ponds and a cottage and following a small brook on your right. Cross a double stile.

11. Follow the path down through the middle of a narrow rough grass area. Cross the stile to continue along the woodland path which shortly turns left to cross a stream via stepping stones. Walk up the bank to cross a stile.

12. Turn right by the waymarked post then almost immediately right again down the bank to turn left up a sunken path which is quite muddy. About halfway up, cross a stile. At the top keep straight on following the field boundary on your left.

13. Cross a waymarked stile in the field corner. Turn left then right round a field corner still with the boundary on your left. Shortly thereafter continue up a short grass track to cross a wall stile and keep straight on through a gateway and on up the middle of the next long field.

14. Cross the stile at the field corner and keep straight on to cross a stile on your left near the next field corner.

15. Turn right in Uppertown to follow the road for about 250 metres, passing Old School Farm on your right. Just after passing a bungalow on your right, cross a stile by the gate, also on your right.

16. Walk diagonally across the field and in the corner pass a waymarked post, then cross two plank footbridges into the next field. Now follow the field boundary on your right. Cross a stile to keep straight on aiming to the right of a bungalow ahead. Walk down steps and across the road.

17. Keep close to a small wall on your right for a few metres then continue in the same direction, leaving the short driveway where it bends left, to walk under the trees and cross a squeeze stile.

18. Follow the wall on your right up the field. Just below the field corner turn right across the wall (broken) then turn left through a wall gap. Bear left under power lines to join a farm track.

19. Turn right up to and through the farm to follow the track up to the road near Alicehead Farm. Turn right along the road for about 100 metres to turn left at the Footpath sign.

20. Follow the path up the moorland, which in late summer is covered in heather and bracken and is a possible picnic spot. Just before the gate the path turns right to a stile by the waymarked post. Cross the stile.

21. Bear left across the field corner to a squeeze stile (do not go through it) and turn right to follow the wall on your left. Cross the stile in the field corner and keep straight on across the middle of the next field to go through another stile by a gate.

22. Continue in the same direction crossing three fields and three stiles, the wall first on your right then on the left. In the fourth field bear left up to the wall to cross a stile at a shallow right-hand bend.

23. Turn right along the farm track to the road. Turn left up the A632 to pass *The Three Horse Shoes Inn* in Spitewinter. After about 150 metres turn right across the road to go down High Ashes Lane.

24. Follow the Lane for just under ½ mile. Turn left across a cattle grid to walk down the Haslehurst Farm Drive. Pass through the farm gate and immediately turn right

25. Walk up the track, through two gates passing between the barns

26. At the end of the barns continue ahead up the bank.

27. Follow the field boundaries on your right to cross three fields and three stiles. In the fourth field bear right to cross the stile in the field corner. In the fifth field bear slightly right to go through a gateway.

28. Keep straight on across the middle of the next two fields crossing two squeeze stiles. In the third and fourth fields, follow the walls on your left. Go through a gate, a squeeze stile and two more gates onto the road at Birkinlane Farm.

29. Turn right down the road for nearly ¼ mile. Just past the Press Manor Fisheries entrance turn left.

30. Follow the field boundaries on your left across two fields, then bear right up the third field to meet a track and a wall on your right. Cross two stiles and an overgrown track.

31. Go through the farm gate then follow the yard round to the left to go through another gate (please close the gates). Follow a track which turns right up to the road.

32. Turn right up the road for nearly ½ mile, then turn right at the footpath post to go through the squeeze stile.

33. Bear left almost diagonally across the field. Cross the stile, the road and another stile. Follow the wall first on your right then on your left, to cross four fields. The stile in the fourth field is below the corner by the gorse bushes.

34. Cross the narrow road and a stile. Follow the narrow stepped path down the steep bank to cross the stile onto the road. Turn right.

35. After about ¼ mile turn left at a T-junction into Ashover. At the next road junction turn left then, at the *Black Swan Inn*, turn left again back to the car park.

BAKEWELL – OVER HADDON

**Bakewell – River Wye – Haddon Park – Haddon Fields –
Lathkill Dale – Over Haddon – Ditch Cliff – Bakewell**

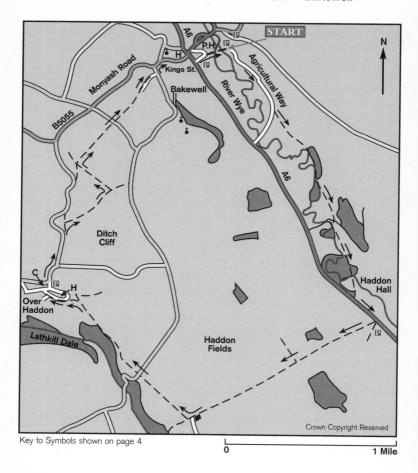

Key to Symbols shown on page 4

0   1 Mile

MAP: O.S. Outdoor Leisure 24 The Peak District White Peak Area.

PARKING: Grid Ref. SK221684

DIRECTIONS: Follow the A6 Matlock to Bakewell road. About 1 mile past Haddon Hall and as you enter Bakewell, turn right signed 'Parking for the town centre, Agricultural Centre, Bakewell Show'. Follow the Agricultural Way to the pay and display car park.

WALK DESCRIPTION:
The walk starts in the interesting market town of Bakewell, where you will find many antique shops, craft shops, cafés, etc. The Bakewell Show is held on the first Wednesday and Thursday in August and the cattle market is every Monday. After leaving the car park the route follows the flat Wye Valley, which may be muddy after heavy rainfall. After passing Haddon Hall (open to the public between April and September) the bridleway and paths gradually climb up above the beautiful Lathkill Dale. In Over Haddon you pass The Lathkill Hotel, a suitable refreshment stop, and Lathkill Dale Working Craft Centre. The return route brings you into the centre of Bakewell.

ROUTE INSTRUCTIONS:
1. From the car park walk back down the Agricultural Way. Where the road bends right keep straight on following the fence and trees close on your left. Cross the stile. Continue ahead following the hedge on your left.
2. On reaching a belt of trees cross a footbridge to follow the riverside path through the trees. Cross the stile at the end of the wood and keep straight on for a few metres before bearing left up the bank to continue in the same direction above the river.
3. After just over 1 mile from the start pass through a gate and turn right down a lane for about 30 metres then turn left over a metal stile.
4. Continue to follow the riverside path through the wood. Cross the bridge over the Wye and then on up the path to cross the stile onto the A6.
5. Turn left down the road. Just before the Haddon Hall car park cross the busy road with care to go through a gate. Pass the car park on your left then go through another gate.
6. Follow the stoney bridleway uphill keeping the wall on your left. Go through a gate. Continue in the same direction, following the field boundaries on your left, to cross three large fields, one gate and one stile.
7. In the third field pass the farm and go through a gate in the field corner. Bear very slightly right across the next field, walk towards the white building at the right-hand end of Over Haddon village. Cross

the stile by the waymarked post and keep straight on aiming for the stile to the left of a field gap.

8. Pass through the squeeze stile, cross the lane and through another squeeze stile. Keep straight on to cross a double stile.

9. Follow the path above the Lathkill river (a lovely picnic spot). Cross a fence stile and bear left up the field aiming for the waymarked post. Cross a stile and go through a small gate. Continue uphill towards the right-hand end of the white building (*The Lathkill Hotel*).

10. Cross the stile. Walk down the road in front of the hotel. Take the right hand fork uphill to join another road and continue ahead to the road junction. Turn right to pass the craft centre and keep straight on along the road out of Over Haddon.

11. After nearly ½ mile and having passed the road to Youlgreave, leave the road where it bends left and keep straight on through a squeeze stile.

12. Walk down the steep slope to cross a gated stile. Turn right to walk towards and past the footpath post. Follow the path as it gradually descends to the valley bottom.

13. Follow the wall on your left, cross a broken wall, down the valley until you reach a gated stile on your left. Go through the gate and turn left.

14. Walk up the field following a wall now on your right. Pass through a squeeze stile in the field corner. Keep straight on, a wall is now on your left. As you near the field corner turn right to walk towards old stone gate posts and follow the hedge on your left.

15. Cross the stile in the field corner. Turn left for a few metres then turn right to follow the hedge on your left. Cross the stile in the field corner. Keep straight on passing the school on your right. Cross the stile and turn right onto the road.

16. Cross the road. Walk down past the tennis courts. At the corner of the playing field keep straight on to follow bushes on your right. Cross the stile.

17. Continuing in the same direction walk down the pavement, across the estate road and on down the path between the houses. The path narrows before widening out into a minor road. Where the road bends right keep straight on down steps. Turn left down the road.

18. At the T-junction turn right down Monyash Road and King's Street, passing the parish church on your left. At the junction with the A6 turn right.

19. Cross the road at the pedestrian crossing and continue down the A6 to take the next left turn. Walk past a car park, the Police Station and the Bakewell Mill Shop. Where the road bends left, fork right across the paved area. Cross two bridges back to the car park.

BIRCHEN EDGE – CHATSWORTH

Birchen Edge – Wellington Monument – Baslow – Chatsworth Park – Hunting Tower – Dobb Edge – Robin Hood Inn

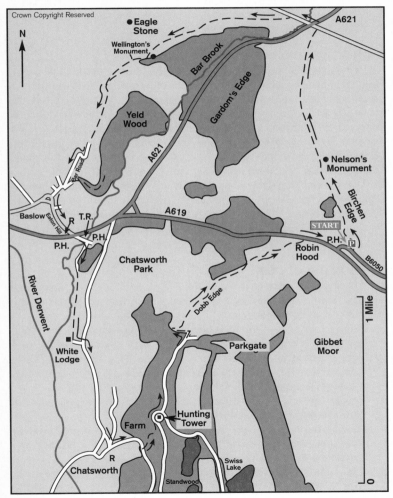

Key to Symbols shown on page 4

MAP: O.S. Outdoor Leisure 24 The Peak District White Peak Area.

PARKING: Grid Ref. SK280721

DIRECTIONS: From Baslow take the A619 Chesterfield / Sheffield road. At the roundabout continue along the A619 Chesterfield road for just over 1 mile. At the Robin Hood Inn turn left onto the B6050 then almost immediately turn left into the car park.

WALK DESCRIPTION:

No Derbyshire walk book would be complete without a visit to Chatsworth Park. This is one of the more spectacular routes which starts up Birchen Edge. Nelson's Monument, perched on the top of the Edge, is 1,000ft. above sea level. It was erected in 1810 only five years after the battle of Trafalgar. Behind the monument are three large stones carved with the names of ships – *Victory*, *Defiant* and *Royal Soverin* (sic) (seen from Dobb Edge). Along the opposite edge you will pass Wellington's Monument, erected in 1866 to commemorate his visit to the Duke of Rutland. From Baslow, where there are a number of inns and tea rooms, the route enters Chatsworth Park. The house, restaurant and craft shops are open from March to October. 148 steps take you up through the woods to the Hunting Tower. From here you follow estate roads and the Dobb Edge concessionary path back to Birchen Edge car park.

ROUTE INSTRUCTIONS:

1. Leave the car park to return to the B6050 and turn left. After about 100 metres and just past a house on the left turn left. Walk up the bank to go through a gate.
2. Keep straight on up the wide steps. Follow the wellused path round to the left. Pass the golf course on your left. Ignore a path on your right and continue to follow the wall on your left. After about ⅓ mile from the road the path bears away from the wall and fence up towards the edge. Ignore another smaller path on the right.
3. Follow the rocky path below Birchen Edge. Soon you will see Nelson's Monument up on your right.
4. Nearing the northern end of Birchen Edge the path veers left away from the edge and winds its way down through the heather and across the moorland. This last stretch could be quite wet.
5. Cross the stile and turn left to cross the A621. Walk up the minor road for about 200 metres. At the top of the hill turn left through a small gate and immediately turn right onto a track by the 'Boundary of

open Country' sign.

6. Follow the track with the high wall on your right. This is the ancient 'CHESTERFEILD ROADE' as you will see on a stone pillar.

7. Where the wall ends keep straight on to the Wellington Monument, noticing the Eagle Stone on your right. About ¾ mile from the minor road you will reach the Wellington Monument. This is a favourite picnic spot.

8. From the monument continue along the track for about 150 metres and at a T-junction of tracks turn left.

9. Follow the wide stoney track downhill to go through a gate. Continue down the walled and hedged track for nearly ½ mile to meet the surfaced road of Bar Road.

10. Walk down Bar Road, passing two roads off left and right, for about 250 metres to the grass island at the junction of School Lane and Bar Road, turn to the left.

11. Walk down Eaton Hill into Nether End, Baslow. Cross the main A619 Turn left along the minor road to pass *Goose Green Tea Rooms* on your left then cross the bridge and turn right into the Chatsworth Estate.

12. Follow the track past the cottages to go through a stile by the left-hand gate of two gates. Continue along the track to go through the Cannon Kissing Gate.

13. Keep straight on following a well-used path above the Bar Brook, to join a surfaced path. When you reach White Lodge, in about 500 metres, turn left up the short tree-lined road.

14. At the T-junction turn right to follow the estate road for about ½ mile. At a fork of roads take the left-hand fork to walk up towards the Chatsworth stables, now a very well run restaurant and craft shop (open March-October). When you reach the T-junction turn left to pass the stable block over to your right.

15. Cross a cattle grid and pass Chatsworth Farmyard on your left. Follow the estate road as it bears right up through the wood signed 'Stand Wood Walks'. After about 100 metres opposite an old building and just before four coloured arrows on a low stone on the left-hand side of the road, turn left.

16. Walk up a narrow woodland path through the laurels and rhododendrons. Cross a wider track diagonally left and continue up the winding narrow path, crossing a stream and walking round a large yew tree to the steps.

17. Climb the 148 steps to the Hunting Tower.

18. Turn left to follow the road round the tower. At a crossing of roads

turn left still on a surfaced road through the woods.

19. After about ⅓ of a mile, and where the road bends right up to a large shed, keep straight on along a farm track for a few metres.

20. Just before a gateway turn left through the wood following the wall on your right. Cross the high wall stile. Turn right then left to follow the wall on your right. From here you can see Nelson's Monument and the 'Three Ships'.

21. After about 300 metres and before the wall corner, the path bears left down to cross another high stile. Keep straight on up the field to walk along the concessionary path of Dobb Edge. Cross the stile in the field corner.

22. Follow the narrow winding rocky and undulating concessionary path. You will cross two stiles. After about 400 metres at the end of Dobb Edge cross a ladder stile.

23. Bear left downhill following the waymarked post and crossing a wider track, then on down steps to cross a planked bridge. Climb the steps to the road.

24. Cross the busy A619 and turn right back to *The Robin Hood* and Birchen Edge car park.

WALK 4 - CASTLETON

6½ MILES

CASTLETON – HOPE

**Peak Cavern – Speedwell Cavern – Knowlegates Farm –
Mam Farm – Woodseats – Hollowford Road Training Centre –
Losehill – Hope – Peakshole Water – Castleton**

MAP: O.S. Outdoor Leisure 1 The Peak District Dark Peak Area.

DIRECTIONS AND CAR PARKING: Park in the centre of Castleton, the car park is off the A6187 at the bottom of Cross Street. Grid Ref. SK149830

WALK DESCRIPTION:

A pleasant easy walk in the foothills and valleys between Hope and Castleton. Much of the route is well signed and follows clear paths and tracks. Take care following instruction 9 so that you do not miss the turn off the main path (which goes up to Hollins Cross and Mam Tor). Castleton and Hope are well worth a visit. There are many souvenir shops, cafés and restaurants.

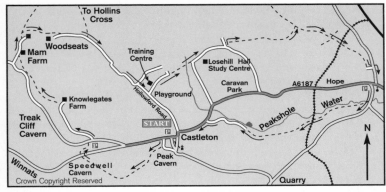

Key to Symbols shown on page 4

0 _____ 1 Mile

ROUTE INSTRUCTIONS:

1. From the car park return to the main road and cross it to follow the minor road between the gift shops and cafés signed 'Riverside Walk to Peak Cavern'.

2. At the road junction turn right across the bridge then on up the hill. The road runs into a track after the last house. Go through a gate.

3. Follow a path with the wall on your right across the bottom of two large fields. Pass through a small gate below the Speedwell Cavern entrance.

4. Cross the road to go over a stile by a gate. Keep straight on for a few metres then turn right to follow a path down to and through a car park. Turn right along the road for a short way then take the first track on the left signed 'The National Trust and Derbyshire Soaring Club' and 'Dunscar Farm'.

5. After nearly 100 metres and just before a cattle grid turn left. Follow the track for another ¼ mile to Knowlegates Farm.

6. Turn left up and around the farm going through a gate and over a stile. Bear left to follow a path up through the bracken and crossing one stile.

7. Near the top by the old mine spoils, bear round the mound aiming for the stile below the bracken (do not go through the wood). Cross the stile to continue on up the grass path which soon leaves the bracken to cross the hillside towards Mam Farm and pass through a fence gap.

8. Walk up to the left-hand end of the farm and cross a stile. Cross a

17

farm track then immediately turn right to follow another track behind the farm. After about 100 metres and before two large properties, turn left over a stile onto National Trust Property.

9. Follow a clear path uphill round the properties and cross a fence stile. Just past the end of the last building on your right leave the main path, which climbs steeply uphill, and turn right.

10. The path is not obvious. You should aim to contour the hillside, keeping a fence down on your right through the trees and crossing a boggy area before you leave the trees to cross two stiles and continue in the same direction to cross a broken wall.

11. Follow a clearer path round the hillside crossing a few small boggy areas above and past Woodseats Farm until you reach a footpath post. Cross the stile.

12. Turn left along a track for just over 300 metres where it turns right to become Hollowford Road. Follow this meandering road for just over ½ mile until you reach a T-junction by the 'Playground' sign and the Hollowford Centre.

13. Turn left to pass the Training Centre and follow a track signed 'Rotary'. After about ¼ mile and having crossed a cattle grid, turn right.

14. Follow the field boundary on your right and where it ends keep straight on to cross stepping stones, go through a small gate and follow the path up to cross another stile by a gate.

15. Keep straight on up a partly-surfaced track behind Losehill Training Centre. Follow this track for about ¼ mile to Spring House.

16. Turn left signed 'Losehill and Hope'. At the top of the driveway go through a small gate and turn right behind the barn to pass through two more small gates. Continue ahead to the end of the hedge on your right and go through the fourth small gate on the right and turn left.

17. Continue in more or less the same easterly direction across six fields, four gates, and one stile, all clearly signed. In the seventh field by a waymarked post and the Footpath sign to Mam Tor via Lose Hill turn right signed 'Hope'.

18. Cross two fields and two gates then follow a track for a few metres before turning right then left through the hedge gap to follow the field boundary on your left.

19. Pass through a gate (do not turn right). Keep straight on to walk behind the house. Go through the squeeze stile then on to cross a stile and over the railway to cross the next stile.

20. Continue ahead in a south easterly direction across five small fields and gates.

21. Turn left along the road and at the T-junction turn right down Edale road to the A6 in Hope, where you turn right then, in a few metres, left, down Pindale Road.

22. After about 250 metres, turn right by a small decorated millstone to cross a stile onto the path above Peakshole Water.

23. Follow this path for about ½ mile crossing four stiles and the railway. After the railway crossing the river meanders away from the path which keeps straight on to pass a short stretch of fence on your right and a waymarked post on your left. Cross the fifth stile and continue ahead crossing four more stiles, a broken wall and five fields.

24. After the fourth stile the path leads into a track which takes you down to the main road.

25. Turn left to walk back into Castleton. The road turns left then right to go down Cross Street back to the car park.

WALK 5 - COMBS RESERVOIR, NR. WHALEY BRIDGE   7 MILES

COMBS RESERVOIR – ECCLES PIKE

Combs Reservoir – Tunstead Milton – Hilltop – Horwich Farm – Roosdyche – Buxworth – Eccles Pike – Lidgate – Bradshaw Hall Farm – Cockyard – Golf Course – Combs Reservoir

MAP: O.S. Outdoor Leisure 24 and 1 The Peak District White Peak and Dark Peak

PARKING: Grid Ref. SK034798

DIRECTIONS: From Buxton take the A5004 Whaley Bridge road. After 6½ miles, at the traffic lights in Horwich turn right onto the B5470 to Chapel and Tunstead Milton. In another 2 miles in Tunstead Milton and having passed *The Rose and Crown Inn* on your left and just after a left-hand bend sign and before the (50) sign turn sharp right at the Combs Reservoir sign and a cul-de-sac sign. Drive down the narrow lane below the reservoir embankment for about 250 metres and turn right into a car park (there is no 'P' sign).

WALK DESCRIPTION:
If you wish for a quiet walk along country tracks and roads in a less popular area – then this route is for you. Some of the climbs are quite steep but you will be rewarded with superb open views up north to the

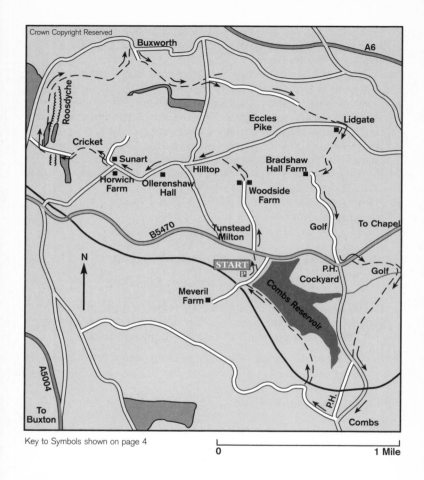

Key to Symbols shown on page 4

0   1 Mile

High Peak and west to Lyme Park. There are refreshment stops in Tunstead Milton, Cockyard and Combs.

ROUTE INSTRUCTIONS:

1. Leave the car park and turn left back down the lane for about 100 metres to where there is a gap in the crash barrier on your left. Walk down the steps and follow a narrow path through an area of mixed meadow plants. Shortly the path turns left under the trees by the reservoir outflow before bending right up to a stile. Cross the stile to

walk up the field bearing very slightly left. Cross a stile by the metal footpath sign.

2. Cross the road to follow the 'Bugsworth via Hill Top Farm' sign. Walk up the partly-surfaced track to walk through Sparkbottom (now converted to private dwellings) then on up to Woodside Farm. Continue ahead following the waymarked signs up the grass track passing a barn on your left to go round a gate. At the next metal sign bear left as indicated to go through a gate.

3. Bear right up the field to cross a stile then keep straight on up the next steep field. Cross the stile and turn left along the minor road.

4. Follow this road for about ¾ mile, passing Ollerenshaw Hall, to Horwich Farm. Where the road turns sharp left, keep straight on up a lane which shortly turns sharp right passing 'Sunart'. Turn left over a stile by a garage.

5. Follow a farm track up the field keeping a wall close on your left. Pass through a walled kissing gate and keep straight on following the wall. Where the wall bends left cross the track to go over a stile.

6. Follow the fence on your left passing the cricket ground on your right. Enter a tree-lined track and pass through a small gate. Continue along the track crossing Roosdyche. Just after passing a footpath sign on the left, turn right over a stile.

7. Keep straight on to go through a gate then continue in the same direction up the field to cross a ladder stile. Keep straight on with a wall on your right to cross another ladder stile. Bear very slightly right to go down and up across Roosdyche. Cross the wall stile ahead.

8. Keep straight on following an old wall on your left. Pass through an old gateway in the field corner and keep straight on down the field passing under power lines to cross a stile beyond a gate.

9. Continue ahead below Mosley Hall Farm to cross a wire and post stile and walk upto a waymarked wall corner. Now follow a wall close on your right to cross a squeeze stile in the field corner then keep straight on to cross a wall stile.

10. Follow an overgrown path down to and through a metal gate, then continue on down the field towards the house. At the garden corner turn right to walk down to and over the stile.

11. Turn sharp right up a surfaced track, passing Western Point Cottage, in Buxworth. At the top of the track continue up a walled path to go through a gate. Turn left.

12. In a few metres you will meet a wall on your right. At the wall corner bear right to walk below the gorse bushes gradually moving downhill towards a belt of trees then aiming for the bottom right-hand corner of

the rough field. Cross the stile by the reeds.

13. Bear off right to meet a wall on your right. Now follow this wall close on your right to climb the steep field. Opposite a ruined house over on your right, turn left across the field aiming for the footpath sign. Cross the stile and a minor road.

14. Walk up a stoney track ignoring a track on your left. Go through a small gate and continue up and along the track for about 400 metres. Cross a stile by a gate and continue along the unfenced track for another ½ mile, crossing the National Trust Eccles Pike moorland.

15. Go through a squeeze stile at Lidgate and turn left down the minor road for about 50 metres. Turn right between conifer hedges by the metal footpath sign. Go through a small gate (there may be a car and caravan here).

16. Turn right to walk past the house and garden. Cross a stile and keep straight on down the field to a wall stile on your right. Cross this stile and walk diagonally down to the opposite field corner. Cross a fence stile and keep straight on down the next field to cross another stile. Turn right to follow the fence and bushes on your right. Cross a squeeze stile.

17. Turn left to follow the garden wall close on your left. Pass the entrance to the impressive Bradshaw Hall Farm. Now follow a partly-surfaced track for nearly ¾ mile passing the golf course.

18. At the B-road in Cockyard, turn left opposite *The Hanging Gate Inn* (a suitable refreshment stop) to walk up the pavement. Just before a drive entrance on your left, in about 200 metres, cross the road to cross a stile by a footpath post.

19. Keep straight on down the field to cross a stile onto the golf course. Follow the waymarked route aiming for a line of old hawthorn trees then cross the fairway to a waymarked post. Turn right to pass a line of trees on your left then bear off left down to a stream to cross a footbridge (not the golfers' bridge). Cross a stile on your right.

20. Keep straight on across the middle of the field to cross another footbridge and stile. Continue ahead along the edge of the golf course to cross a stile and a planked marshy area. Bear left under power lines then bear off right under more power lines. Cross the middle of the next field to pass through a wide fence gap. Turn left following a fence on your left across two fields. Cross a stile by an old gate.

21. Turn left along the road for about 300 metres. Walk under the railway bridge into Combs village. On reaching *The Beehive Inn* (another suitable refreshment stop), turn right, round the inn ignoring a very narrow road on your right to follow a minor narrow road for about

⅓ mile to a gate and waymarked footpath post on your right.

22. Go over the stile by the gate and keep straight on under the railway to follow a hedge on your right. About halfway down the field bear off left to cross a stile under the holly bushes. Now walk diagonally across the middle of the next field to pass under a holly bush and an oak tree. Bear left down the field to cross a footbridge.

23. Turn left to follow a rather muddy path with the reservoir on your right. After a while, the path becomes less muddy and much nearer the reservoir. Cross a footbridge. Near the end of the reservoir cross the side dam wall and so down to the lane and the car park.

WALK 6 - DERBYSHIRE BRIDGE, Nr. BUXTON   6½ MILES

AXE EDGE MOOR – CAT & FIDDLE

Derbyshire Bridge car park – Axe Edge Moor – Dane Head – Orchard Common – Reeve-edge Quarries – Danebower Hollow – Cat & Fiddle

MAP: O.S. Outdoor Leisure 24 The Peak District White Peak Area.

PARKING: Grid Ref. SK019716

DIRECTIONS: From the centre of Buxton take the A53 Leek road, after just over 1 mile turn right onto the A54 and after 1½ miles, take the right-hand fork onto the A537 Macclesfield road. Then, in nearly 300 metres, turn right to follow an unfenced minor road for about ½ mile to a T-junction, turn right and drive for about 300 metres to the car park.

WALK DESCRIPTION:
From Derbyshire Bridge you follow a stoney track before heading across a short moorland path to follow another track. The path across Axe Edge Moor is easy to follow and usually dry. The nearly ½ mile stretch from the minor road at Dane Head to the Derbyshire/Cheshire boundary is not so obvious and can be quite boggy which is why you should only attempt this moorland walk in fine dry weather. The section through the old quarries provides a number of picnic spots. From the A54 to *The Cat & Fiddle Inn* the route is very clear.

ROUTE INSTRUCTIONS:
1. With the toilet block down on your right and with your back to the car park entrance, walk up the stoney track. After about 200 metres and a

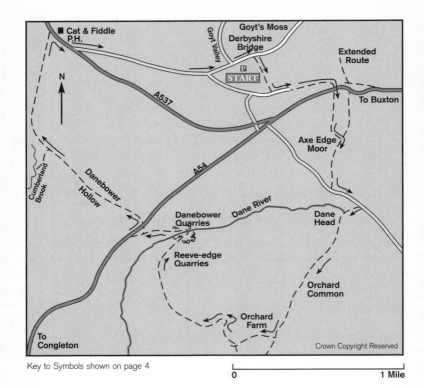

Key to Symbols shown on page 4

0   1 Mile

   right-hand shallow bend, turn right at a low waymarked sign.
2. Follow a moorland path in a SE direction to meet a broken wall on your right. Continue in the same direction to pass through a wall gap and turn right. Follow the track, keeping the broken wall on your left, for nearly ½ mile. After passing a stile on your left and before reaching the main road, turn right across the rough grass to walk towards the footpath sign.
3. Cross the A54 and go over the stile. Keep straight on up Axe Edge Moor walking in a southerly direction. In about 350 metres the path turns left by a broken wall and in another 130 metres, joins a wider path at a T-junction. Turn right to follow this path for nearly ½ mile, still walking mainly south, to join a minor road.
4. Turn left along the unfenced road for about 475 metres. Turn right by a footpath sign.

5. Follow a track in a SW direction for 175 metres and at a waymarked post the track bends to follow a more southerly direction for another 300 metres, before bending right for 150 metres to cross a waymarked old fence stile on the Derbyshire/Cheshire boundary. This stretch can be quite boggy.

6. The track now becomes more obvious. After about ½ mile and below the derelict Orchard Farm up on your right, turn right up the farm drive.

7. Follow the drive as it bends right round the collapsing buildings. Where the stoney driveway bends sharp left downhill, keep straight on.

8. Follow a wide grass path which contours the hillside crossing the head of a small valley via a broken gateway and turning left. Cross a small stream and continue ahead still contouring the hillside. When you meet a wall on your left, follow it for nearly ½ mile.

9. When you reach the wall corner where it turns left steeply downhill, keep straight on still following the grass track. Shortly at a fork of tracks take the left-hand fork.

10. Follow the track down through the old quarry workings to waymarked post. Turn left across the River Dane via stepping stones, then keep straight on up the quarry to a waymarked footpath post. Turn left up a short steep embanked path to the top of the quarry. The path now continues on a wider gradually climbing track to a stile by a gate.

11. Go over the stile and keep straight on along the wide track to the main A54. Turn right and go along the busy road for about 200 metres. (If you wish to avoid the road then turn sharp right immediately after crossing the stile to climb a short very steep path to the crash barrier by the road. Cross the barrier and the road back onto the moorland track.) Turn left back onto the moors.

12. Follow the moorland track across Danebower Hollow for about 1½ miles to the A537 and *The Cat & Fiddle Inn*; ignore a path, coming in on your left, about halfway along this track.

13. Cross the road and turn right at the Inn. Walk down the unfenced main road for 200 metres, then fork left down the minor moorland road which leads back to the car park, in about 1 mile.

If you wish for a longer walk of 12 miles, you can combine Walks 6 and 10.

LUMSDALE - CUCKOOSTONE

Eddlestow Lot – A632 – Lant Lane – Old Engine Farm –
Holestone Moor Farm – Derbyshire Oaks Quarry – Tansley Knoll –
Lumsdale – Bentley Bridge – Cuckoostone Dale –
Cuckoostone Lane – Bottom Moor – Eddlestow Lot

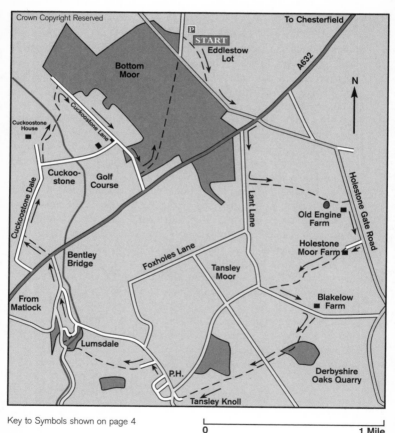

Key to Symbols shown on page 4

0　　　　　　　　　　　　　　1 Mile

MAP: O.S. Outdoor Leisure 24 The Peak District White Peak Area

PARKING: Grid Ref. SK324632

DIRECTIONS: From the Crown island in the centre of Matlock take the A615 signed Motorway M1, Alfreton, Chesterfield, Tansley, Riber. In nearly ½ mile turn left signed A632 Chesterfield. In 2½ miles turn left signed Darley Dale and Beeley. In ½ mile turn right at the sign for Uppertown and Picnic Area 200 yards. Turn right into the car park and picnic area.

WALK DESCRIPTION:
A walk of changing vistas and early industrial archeology. The first part of the route follows undulating field paths and roads, before reaching Tansley Knoll where *The Gate Inn* provides a half-way refreshment stop. Part of the return route is through 'The Arkwright Society Project' where you will climb steps up the beautiful Lumsdale where the mill buildings are clothed in ferns and ivy and waterfalls tumble down the rhododendron-fringed rocky gorge.

ROUTE INSTRUCTIONS:
1. Leave the small car park at the top left-hand corner by a wall under the trees. Follow the well-defined path passing the picnic area in the quarry on your right. Go through the squeeze stile and continue ahead following the wall on your left; there is no clear path. Pass through a gap by a gate to follow the fence on your left. Pass through a small gate and in a few metres cross a stile onto the road.
2. Turn left along the road. At the T-junction with the A632 turn right. After nearly 100 metres turn left, signed Tansley, to walk up Lant Lane for about 500 metres. Turn left through a squeeze stile by the footpath post.
3. Walk up the tree-lined path and through the squeeze stile. Continue in the same direction with the field boundary on your right. Pass through the gateway and on up the next field to go through a squeeze stile. Continue on up towards the farm.
4. At a wall gap turn right to follow the wall on your left. Walk past a small lake on your right then bear left up through a rough area to cross a stile. Walk up the next field toward Old Engine Farm and the field corner.
5. Cross the stile and turn right down Holestone Gate Road for about 350 metres then turn right down Holestone Moor Farm Drive.
6. Walk through the farmyard to cross a waymarked stile. Turn left then right by the waymarked post to cross concrete 'planks'. Keep straight on down the field to go through a gate. Continue in the same direction to the power lines then bear left to follow a wall on your left. Cross the stile in the field corner. Follow an overgrown stream on your right for a

few metres then turn right down a small bank and over the stream and a stile.

7. Follow the wall on your right up three fields and across three stiles (there may be an electric fence and a stile in the third field).

8. Turn left up the road for ¼ mile. Turn right opposite Blakelow Farm and the caravan site.

9. With a wall on your right cross three fields and three stiles. In the fourth field bear left towards the wood. Cross the stile and follow the path through Derbyshire Oaks Quarry to cross another stile. Continue ahead still with the wall on your right.

10. On reaching the lane cross it diagonally right. Walk along the left hand boundary of the next two fields crossing two stiles. Follow the grass path down the next three fields, crossing two stiles.

11. Bear left down a wooded path to cross a stile. Follow the line of the hedge on your right for a very short distance then turn left down a wide stone-edged path. Cross the stile in the field corner and keep straight on down the next two fields, crossing two stiles and keeping the hedge on your right.

12. Turn left to follow a short walled grass track between houses. Turn right down the lane to the crossroads in Tansley Knoll. Keep straight on at the crossroads to follow a narrow road uphill, passing *The Gate Inn* on your right. Continue down through Tansley Knoll for about 250 metres. Cross the bridge and turn left off the road at the 'Lumsdale and Matlock Bank' sign.

13. Walk up a track passing round or through four gates and passing a track on your right. In the first field follow a wall on your right to go through a small gate on your right. Now follow a fence on your left to cross a squeeze stile then cross the next field to go through another squeeze stile. Follow a fenced and walled path past a house to go through the third squeeze stile and continue ahead. Cross two stiles.

14. Turn right up a wooded minor road in Lumsdale. In a few metres turn right through a wall gap into 'The Arkwright Society Lumsdale Project' area. Follow the path and steps up this beautiful valley passing old fern and ivy covered mill buildings and waterfalls. Eventually the path and steps turn away from the second waterfall to follow a low wall and the mill pond on your right.

15. Go through the wall gap, turn left then immediately right to walk past Pond Cottages on your right. Follow a partly-surfaced track for about 300 metres to join a minor road in Bentley Bridge. On reaching the A632 Chesterfield Road, cross it to the Footpath post.

16. Walk up the walled grass path to cross the stile. Follow the wall on your

left and where it ends, bear right down a rough area to go up a small bank keeping the trees on your left. Now keep straight on up the next two fields, passing through a wide gap and then a squeeze stile.

17. Turn right along a partly-metalled track. After just over ¼ mile cross a stile by a gate then bear right off the track to follow a wide grass path downhill under the trees.

18. At the two footpath posts keep straight on ignoring the walled golf club path on your right. Follow the path, which bears off slightly away from the wall on your right, to a waymarked tree. The path now bears right down to the end of a wall. Follow a path, diagonally across the field below Cuckoostone House. Cross a broken wall. Walk down through the bracken, then on down a bank to cross a footbridge and a stile.

19. Climb the rocky wooded path ahead. Cross two stiles. Leave the wood and bear slightly right across the field to cross another stile. Follow a path through a wood to go through a small gateway. Turn right then left to follow the path uphill.

20. At a grass track turn right. In nearly ½ mile pass by a gate and the back of a house to join the partly-surfaced track of Cuckoostone Lane which you follow for another ½ mile.

21. At the end of the wood on your left, turn left signed 'Public Footpath to Robridding'. Follow the path which goes first along the edge of the wood before it curves round to the left to pass through an avenue of conifers. Eventually a path comes in on the left. A few metres further on keep straight ahead at a crossing of paths. Continue up through a more open area of woodland crossing another path. Cross the stile at the end of the wood. This woodland section is about ¾ mile.

23. Cross the road and follow the sign 'Uppertown' and 'Picnic Area 200 yards'. Walk down the road back to the car park.

STOKE FORD – EYAM MOOR

Eyam – Highcliffe – Jubilee Plantation – Stoke Ford – Hazelford – Leadmill – Leam Farm – Eyam Moor – Sir William Hill Road – Eyam

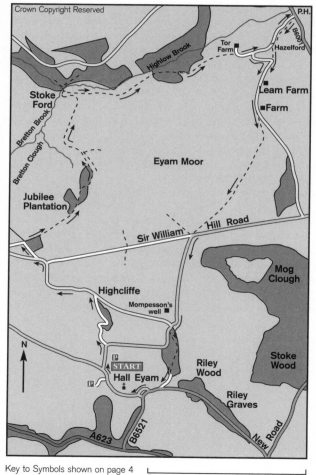

Key to Symbols shown on page 4

0   1 Mile

PARKING: Eyam pay and display car park. Grid Ref. SK216767.

MAP: O.S. Outdoor Leisure 24 The Peak District White Peak Area and Leisure 1 Dark Peak Area.

DIRECTIONS: From Baslow take the A623 to Calver and Stoney Middleton. Drive through these two villages. In about ¾ mile from Stoney Middleton turn right to Eyam on the B6521. At the top of the hill turn left to drive through the village, passing the church on your right and Eyam Hall car park on your left, then the Post Office on your right. Turn right up Hawkhill road signed 'Car Park'.

WALK DESCRIPTION:
A varied walk starting and finishing in Eyam Village where you can visit Eyam Craft Centre and Hall. You will notice plaques on some of the cottage walls describing the plague of 1665. After a steep climb onto Eyam Edge, the walk crosses open moorland before descending to a pretty picnic spot at Stoke Ford. From here the undulating path crosses the northern edge of Eyam Moor before descending to Leadmill and *The Plough Inn* (a suitable refreshment stop). The return route across Eyam Moor brings you to the Sir William Hill Road before descending the road and paths back to the eastern end of Eyam and a pleasant ¼ mile walk through the village to the car park.

ROUTE INSTRUCTIONS:
1. Leave the car park and turn right up the hill. Where the road bends right keep straight on up the road which leads onto a track. This track winds steeply uphill through the woods.
2. On reaching the road at Highcliffe turn left. Follow the road, which bends sharp right, for about ½ mile to the end of the Sir William Hill Road. Follow the minor road round to the left and in about 75 metres turn right onto a gravel track.
3. Follow the track for about 275 metres and opposite a track on your left turn right over the ladder stile signed 'Stoke Ford'.
4. Follow a wide path with a wall on your left passing rhododendrons and Jubilee Plantation. After passing a small low building leave the wall on the left to continue uphill to the top corner of a wood and stone gateposts.
5. Continue ahead along a wide grass path to cross a stile by a gate. Keep straight on following the wall close on your left and going round a right hand bend. Cross a stile by a gate and turn left.
6. Continue to follow the wall and woodland then moorland on your left with the western edge of Eyam Moor up on your right. Cross a stile by a gate in the moorland corner.
7. Follow the wide grass path along the ridge overlooking Bretton

Clough. Cross one stile. Follow the path, as it veers away from the wall on your right and descends in a curve and zig-zag. Near the valley bottom there are two right turns; either one will lead down to Stoke Ford.

8. Opposite the bridge over Bretton Brook at Stoke Ford (do not cross the bridge) bear right uphill away from the Brook.

9. Follow the undulating moorland path crossing a stream, a stile by a gate then following a fence on your left to cross another stile by a gate. Continue on down a wide track through the wood.

10. Cross a small tributary stream ahead to go over a stile.

11. Keep straight on up through the established conifer and silver birch area.

12. Cross a stile and continue in the same direction crossing three fields and going through three gateways.

13. At Tor Farm go through two gates then bear slightly right up the farm drive. On reaching the road you have a choice :-
a) *If you do not wish to have refreshments at The Plough Inn turn sharp right uphill to follow the road for about 250 metres. Here you will bend round to the right to join the route directions at No. 17.*
b) *If you wish to visit The Plough Inn, turn left downhill.*

14. Follow the road down to the B6001 for about ½ mile, then turn left to The Plough Inn. Retrace your steps back to the minor road. Turn up the road for a few metres to cross a stile on your left.

15. Walk up the field with the hedge and minor road on your right. Cross the stile below Hazelford Hall and turn left up the road round the Hall to cross a wall stile on your left.

16. Walk straight up the steep field to enter a sunken path and continue on uphill. Cross the stile onto the road.

17. Keep straight on following the road for nearly ¼ mile passing Leam Cottage and Leam Farm. Turn right opposite the second farm and where the road bends turn left.

18. Cross the stile onto Eyam Moor and turn left. Follow the well-defined path up Eyam Moor. After about ¾ mile you reach a fence on your left. Follow this fence for just over ¼ mile.

19. On reaching a gate cross the stile onto the road. Bear right, passing the end of Sir William Hill Road, to walk down the road towards Eyam. In about ¼ mile you will pass Mompesson's Well and the Abney road on your right. A few metres further on and just past Hollow Brook Barn turn left through a squeeze stile.

20. Follow the path down through the wood. At the end of the wood continue on down Riley Back Lane.

21. On reaching the B6521 road in Eyam turn right and where it bends left keep straight on to walk the ¼ mile back through the village to the car park.

CRESSBROOK DALE – FOOLOW

**Eyam – Tideswell Lane – Housley – Wardlow – Cressbrook Dale –
Wardlow Mires – Stanley House – Foolow – Eyam**

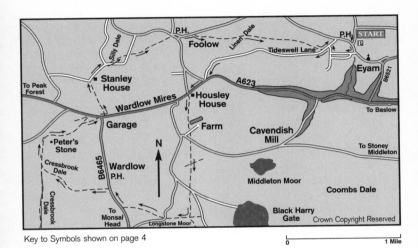

Key to Symbols shown on page 4

0   1 Mile

MAP: O.S. Outdoor Leisure 24 The Peak District White Peak Area.

PARKING: Pay and Display.   Grid Ref. SK216767

DIRECTIONS: From Baslow take the A623 road north to Calver and Stoney Middleton; then take the B6521 on the right signed Eyam, about 3½ miles from Baslow. At the top of the hill turn left to drive through Eyam, passing the church on your right, for about ½ mile then turn right at the car park sign up Hankhill road.

WALK DESCRIPTION:
Although this is one of the longer walks in the book it has relatively easy-to-follow field paths and tracks. The only steep section is the descent into the beautiful grassy Cressbrook Dale where there are many picnic areas. The views across the rolling open countryside are spectacular, especially from the edge of Longstone Moor. Eyam, the plague village of 1665, is well described in the many books on Derbyshire. Eyam was one of the

first villages in the country to have a public water system for in 1588 twelve sets of stone troughs were built and spring water from the base of Eyam Edge was piped to them. Some of these troughs are still to be seen in the village. *The Bull's Head Inn* in Foolow, 1½ miles west of Eyam offers a suitable refreshment stop about three-quarters of the way round the route.

ROUTE INSTRUCTIONS:

1. Leave the car park and turn left back down the road. At the T-junction turn left, passing the Post Office and opposite the entrance to Eyam Hall Craft Centre turn right down New Close. Keep straight on up the hill, cross the road and follow the surfaced path up between the houses to cross another road. At the top of the hill go through the squeeze stile.

2. Cross the lane diagonally right to go through a wall gap. Walk across the field to go through another wall gap.

3. Turn left up Tideswell Lane. After the last bungalow the lane becomes a stoney track. Follow this winding, undulating walled track for about 1¼ miles.

4. At the road junction turn left then right to follow the A623 for nearly 300 metres. At Housley House, opposite the minor road to Foolow, turn left to cross the stile on your right.

5. Turn left to walk through a rough area passing a dew pond on your right. Follow a wall on your left to cross one and perhaps two stiles.

6. Keep straight on up the next two fields crossing two stiles. Walk diagonally across the next field to cross a stile and a farm drive and another stile.

7. Bear right to cross a stile, a road and low ladder stile.

8. Bear slightly left up the middle of the next large field. Cross the stile. Bear right to walk up to and over the next stile 50 metres to the left of a tree in the field corner. Bear left up the field.

9. Cross a fence stile and keep straight on to cross two more stiles (one of these stiles may be temporary).

10. Cross a track to go through a small gate. Bear slightly right across the next two fields, cross a broken wall and going through another small gate, cross the road and stile.

11. Continue ahead crossing three fields and three stiles.

12. Turn right down the edge of Longstone Moor, follow the wall on your right and cross a stile in the field corner.

13. Cross the road and stile. Keep straight across two fields and over two stiles.

14. Keep straight on contouring the hillside. Pass a power line pole on

your right then follow a broken wall on your right. Continue up the field, now with a main wall close on your right, to cross a stile by a gate.

15. Turn right down the road into Wardlow. After about 300 metres, near the bottom of the hill turn left at the 'Public Footpath to Ravensdale' sign.

16. Follow the walled path and where it bends right go through the stile ahead. Keep straight on up the long, very narrow field.

17. Cross the stile into Cressbrook Dale (managed by English Nature). Turn right to follow a steep path down into the dale. Continue on up the grassy dale for about ¾ mile.

18. At the top of the dale go through a farm gate and walk behind a stone barn. Turn left down to the main road, turn right for about 100 metres, then turn left and cross the road opposite the garage car parking area.

19. Walk down the short farm drive, turn left then right round a large barn. Go through the gate.

20. Follow a wall on your left up two fields and over two stiles. Then bear slightly left up the next field to Stanley House. Go over the stile by the gate in the field corner.

21. Turn right to follow a track for about 325 metres. Keep straight on where the track turns left. Walk down the narrower track. At the bottom of Silly Dale turn left over a stile.

22. Follow the wall on your right uphill to go through a gateway. Keep straight on across the middle of two fields. Cross a track. Cross the next field diagonally, go over the stile and bear left up the field to cross a broken wall.

23. Keep straight on crossing four fields, three stiles and a gate. Turn right down the fifth field to go through a gate by the houses.

24. Walk down a short track, then a very narrow path into Foolow. Pass the duck pond and *The Bull's Head Inn* on your left to walk down the Eyam road. In about 200 metres, at the 'Foolow' road sign, turn right over a stile.

25. Bear very slightly left across the field towards a ruin. Cross two squeeze stiles below the ruin which is up on your right.

26. Now keep straight on walking in an easterly direction to cross 19 small fields and crossing stiles, broken walls and two farm tracks. In the fifth field you cross Linen Dale.

27. After the last stile walk along a narrow hedged and walled path to go down steps onto Tideswell Lane. Turn left to follow the lane down to the T-junction.

28. Turn right to walk back into Eyam, then turn left back to the car park.

GRINLOW – AXE EDGE MOOR

Grinlow – Stanley Moor Reservoir – Turncliff – Leap Edge – A53 – Axe Edge Moor – A54 – Burbage – Grin Plantation – Grinlow

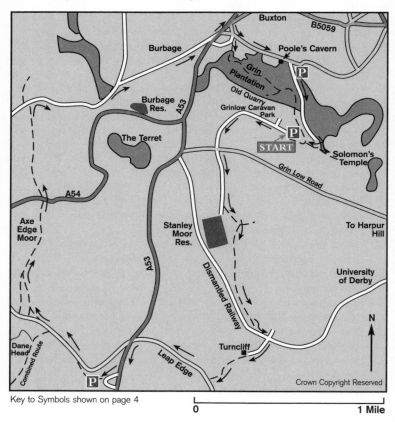

Key to Symbols shown on page 4

0　　　　　　　　　　　　　　　　　1 Mile

MAP: O.S. Outdoor Leisure 24 The Peak District White Peak Area.

PARKING: Grid Ref. SK049720

DIRECTIONS: From the centre of Buxton take the A53 Leek road. After about 1½ miles turn left off the main road signed Harper Hill. In about 250 metres turn left at the caravan and parking sign. Follow the driveway across the cattle grid and up the hill and on down to the car park.

WALK DESCRIPTION:
A walk of great contrast between the magnificent sweeping vistas of the moors south west of Buxton and the leafy woodland tracks of Grin Woods near Burbage. If you wish to visit Solomon's Temple and Poole's Cavern, you will add about half a mile onto your walk. Solomon's Temple was built 1440 ft. above sea level in 1896 by Solomon Mycock to provide work for the unemployed. Poole's Cavern is famous for its unique stalactites and stalagmites. It is electrically lit and has only 16 steps. The cavern can also be reached from Green Lane off the main Buxton road in Burbage. Buxton, a spa town, is well worth a visit. There are splendid gardens, a museum, many gift shops and the famous Buxton Opera House.

ROUTE INSTRUCTIONS:
1. Leave the car park at the entrance and retrace your route back to the road. Cross the road by the two Public Footpath signs.
2. Pass a 'Private' bar gate and go through a metal gate to follow a gravel track. After about 600 metres you will meet the reservoir boundary wall on your right. Just after the wall corner walk up a tarmac stretch of track for a few metres then leave the surfaced track to walk up a wide grass track on your right.
3. Follow this track for about ½ mile crossing a broken wall and passing Anthony Hill up on your left. At the end of this hill and with the line of the old railway track on your right leave the wide grass track to follow a path down on your right towards a wood. Follow a broken wall on your left walking down then up crossing a stream and then a broken wall. Go through a kissing gate.
4. Follow a path uphill through the trees.
5. On reaching a surfaced track turn left for about 150 metres. At a crossroads turn right up a tarmac drive. Walk behind the stone building at Turncliff.
6. Keep straight on signed Brand Side via Leek Road. The tarmac track now becomes a stone and grass track. Cross a stile by a metal gate and climb steeply up through an open stand of trees to Leap Edge. At the top of the track go through an old kissing gate.
7. Turn right along the minor road for nearly ½ mile. Then turn left down the A53 for nearly 300 metres to turn right into the car park (a suitable picnic spot).
8. Walk to the back of the car park to cross a stile then follow a grass

path up the valley to join a minor unfenced road and turn left.

9. After about ¼ mile and having passed a footpath sign on your left, turn right at the DVW and Public Footpath signs.

10. Follow the path up the moorland and on joining another path turn right and continue across Axe Edge Moor. On reaching the next, more stoney, track at a T-junction turn right again. Follow this track down to the A54.

11. Cross the busy main road and walk down a narrow path to cross a stile.

12. Keep straight on following a grass and stone track to join another track coming in on the left. Continue up the moorland away from the main road. After about ½ mile cross a stile.

13. Turn right, down a wide stoney track. After nearly 1 mile this track becomes a minor road through Burbage. After another ½ mile and having ignored all side roads you will see the traffic lights.

14. Just before the traffic lights, turn right past the war memorial column and cross the A53 Leek road. Turn left to cross a minor road, Green Lane, leading to Church View Cottages, then keep straight on signed 'Poole's Cavern and Country Park'. At the *Duke of York Inn* on your left, turn right up Duke Street to pass the Post Office and a road on your left, Green Lane. If you wish to visit Poole's Cavern for a 45 minute conducted tour, keep straight on round the left-hand bend passing Holmfield Road on the right and the 'Playground' sign on the left. After nearly ½ mile you will reach Poole's Cavern Visitor Centre and car park. To return to Grin Low car park follow the signs to Solomon's Temple, climbing the steps at the back of the car park and turn left up the main track through Grin Woods ignoring all side paths. At the top of the track turn left for Solomon's Temple. Turn right for the car park following the wall on your right to climb steps and go through a small gate and turn left. Now follow instruction 19. If, however, you wish to return to the car park without these visits, turn up Holmfield road. After about 50 metres turn left at a footpath sign.

15. Walk up a short track then a short path. By the gate into the children's play area, turn right up two steps to enter the woodland.

16. Follow a well-defined path through the trees, then follow a wall on your left. At the wall corner turn left and continue to follow a broken wall on your left. Where this broken wall turns left downhill, stay on the main path. A few metres further on branch off up to the right at a fork of paths. Ignore all side paths and continue on an uphill path. After a right-hand bend by some raspberry bushes you meet a wider path. Follow this uphill to join another path coming in on the right.

Continue uphill. At a meeting of paths turn left over a small low rock outcrop. Keep straight on ignoring all side paths (this stretch may be muddy).

17. When you reach steps up the hillside on your right, turn right to climb them. Continue along the path and at a fork of paths take the right-hand one up the hill to a fence corner. Here the narrow path turns left to follow the fence on your right.

18. On reaching a gate go through a gap by the gate to leave the wood. Ignore the small gate up on your left, unless you wish to visit Solomon's Temple.

19. Keep straight on between the rock outcrops. After about 100 metres turn right down the quarry path back to the car park.

WALK 11 - HULME END, Nr. HARTINGTON   7½ MILES

HULME END – BRUND

Hulme End – Brund – Pool – Blake Brook –
Cuckoostone – Hayes – Hulme End

MAP: O.S. Outdoor Leisure 24 The Peak District White Peak Area.

PARKING: Grid Ref. SK103593

DIRECTIONS: From Ashbourne take the A515 Buxton road. After 12 miles turn left to follow the B5054 for 2½ miles into Hartington. Continue to follow the B5054, signed Warslow, for about 2 miles. Turn left into the Hulme End pay and display car park by The Manifold Valley Visitor Centre.

WALK DESCRIPTION:
If you wish for a quiet walk with long extensive views over the rolling countryside of the Peak National Park in north east Staffordshire then this route is for you. The route follows country lanes and tracks and little-used paths through small hamlets. Short stretches of the route can be quite muddy so it is advisable to choose a period of dry weather. The Manifold Valley Visitor Centre and Hartington are well worth a visit. Picnic areas are best found off the track below Revidge. Hartington is a very interesting large village with many refreshment places, craft shops and the famous cheese shop.

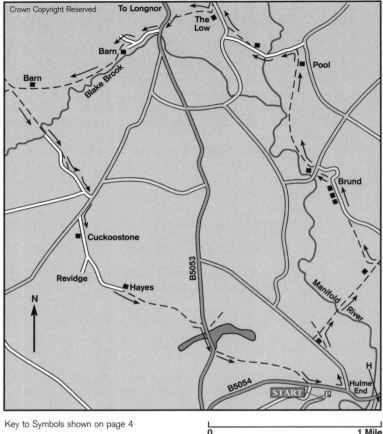

Key to Symbols shown on page 4

0   1 Mile

ROUTE INSTRUCTIONS:

1. Leave the car park and return to the road. Turn right back into the hamlet of Hulme End. Turn left just before the village shop and walk up the minor road for about ½ mile. Turn right at the footpath sign to cross the stile.

2. Bear left to cross another stile at a field corner. Follow the hedge close on your right to cross a squeeze stile in the field corner then almost immediately cross the stile on your right. Keep straight on down the field and down a bank to cross a squeeze stile by a gate. Continue ahead following the fence on your right to cross a footbridge

40

over the River Manifold.

3. Keep straight on skirting the undercut bend of the river on your left before walking across the field to follow a hedge on your right. Cross the squeeze stile in the field corner. Follow the field boundary close on your left.

4. When the wall ends at a waymarked gatepost turn left, passing a gate on the left to go through a waymarked squeeze stile by another gate. Walk through a small copse of trees to cross another stile.

5. Continue ahead following the wall on your right to cross two fields and two stiles, then follow a very short walled track across a stream. Keep straight on to join a farm track. Cross a stile by a gate.

6. Turn left along the lane into the hamlet of Brund. Just before the lane bends sharp right, cross the stile on your left.

7. Bear right down the field walking through a widely-spaced line of posts, and parallel to the road and stream down on your right. Descend the bank to cross the stream and turn left across a marshy area to the wall stile and footpath post. Cross the stile onto the road and turn right for a few metres following the road round to the left where it is joined by another road coming in on the right.

8. Cross the stile on your left at the end of the garden wall. Follow the narrow fenced and walled path, passing the gardens, to cross a stile.

9. Follow the broken wall on your right and where it ends keep straight on to pass through a gateway and follow a wide, fenced, walled and tree-lined track for a short way before it opens out into a field. Keep straight on with the field sloping upon your right and pass a waymarked post. Cross a waymarked stile in the field corner.

10. Turn right to follow the field boundary on your right. Cross a stile and keep straight on to meet the River Manifold on your left. Pass a waymarked post on your right then bear right up the bank to another waymarked post. This whole area is rather indeterminate and muddy.

11. Walk up the next field to cross a squeeze stile then keep straight on across the middle of the next two fields crossing a wall stile. Cross two stiles and a stream. Follow the hedge on your left to cross a squeeze stile and keep straight on, passing an old railway wagon and buildings at Pool.

12. Go through a waymarked gate and follow the path down the bank over a footbridge and through another gate. Walk up to a stile on your right (do not cross it) and then on through a hedge gap to follow the hedge on your right. Cross the stile.

13. Turn left down a walled and hedged track. Cross a stile by a gate and keep straight on to pick up a fence on your left. Go through the small

gate ahead and cross the footbridge.

14. Turn right up the farm track and through the yard to go through a gate ahead. Turn right through the squeeze stile.

15. Turn left up the field to follow the field boundary on your left for a short way then bear right to pass through a squeeze stile between a fence and a gate. Bear right up the next field to go through another squeeze stile by a gate in the top field corner.

16. Turn right up the lane for about 250 metres. After passing the buildings of The Low turn left through a gate or the squeeze. Bear left back towards the farm wall then turn right to pass three large barns on your left. At the power line pole bear right across the field aiming for a farm on the opposite hillside. (The path is not obvious!). As you descend this steep field you will see a footbridge ahead of you.

17. Cross the footbridge and keep straight on up the field to cross a squeeze stile and turn right to cross a stile by a gate.

18. Turn left down the B5053. After about 200 metres bear right down a track, just before a bridge and by a house and footpath sign.

19. Follow the stoney track with Blake Brook on your left for about 125 metres where you bend round to the right to go through a gate by a footbridge (not the gate ahead). Continue up the walled and fenced track for a few more metres then go through the squeeze stile on your left.

20. Bear right towards a stone barn. Cross the wall stile and pass the barn on your left. Follow the wall on your left and cross the stile by a gate in the field corner.

21. Bear right up a small bank then turn left to walk along the top of the gorse bank above the marsh until you reach a wall corner on your right (about 200 metres).

22. Follow a wall on your right walking away from the brook. Cross a stile in the field corner.

23. Keep straight on across the middle of the field walking towards a stone barn. Pass the barn/animal pens on your right to cross a fence stile and footbridge.

24. Keep straight on across the rough marshy field. You will soon see a small grass bank on your left and one at right angles to it on your right. Follow the bank on your left for a few metres until you reach a line of small trees (hawthorn). Turn left to follow the trees on your right.

25. At the end of these trees turn left towards a single tree and on down the field to cross a stile by a gate. Turn right down the field to cross a fence stile by a gate and a stream.

26. Follow the wall on your right down the rough field. Cross a fence stile

on your right and turn left across the footbridge over Blake Brook.

27. Keep straight on up, following the wall on your right, to meet a track. Follow the track uphill to cross the right-hand stile of two stiles on your left by a gate across the track. Continue up the track for just over 100 metres and where it bends right keep straight on across a small area of rough grass to cross a wall stile.

28. Walk up the field to the right-hand end of a stone barn. Cross a squeeze stile under the trees and turn right following the wall on your right to go through another squeeze stile back onto the track.

29. Turn left to follow the track for about 250 metres to the road.

30. Turn right along the road and after nearly ¼ mile turn left up a minor road passing Cuckoostone. At the top, cross the cattle grid and bear round to the left to follow the wide stone track skirting the lower slopes of Revidge (a good picnic spot). The track descends to Hayes Farm.

31. At the yard entrance bear right to a waymarked post. Go through the gate then bear left to go through a gap in the field corner. (The exact route may change depending on how the farmer arranges his gates.)

32. Follow the wall on your right to enter a short walled track by the footpath sign. Go through a gate. Bear right to walk diagonally down the large rough field ahead aiming for the left-hand end of a wood. Pass through a waymarked gate above the field corner.

33. Keep straight on down the field to a wall corner then on down to another wall corner. Follow the wall on your left until you reach a gate on the left, go through it and follow the track down to the road.

34. Turn right along the B5053 for about 230 metres. At the end of the wood on the left and opposite a footpath sign on the right turn left to cross a stile by a gate.

35. Walk down a very short track then turn right to pass a waymarked power line pole. Walk almost diagonally across the large field towards a gate. Cross the stile. Keep straight on above the small valley on your right. There may be a fence on your left. Pass a group of three trees (sycamore and beech) on your right to cross a brook by an old stone gatepost.

36. Continue ahead across the middle of the next field and cross a squeeze stile. Keep straight on to cross a farm track (you may have to cross a stile over an electric fence). Continue ahead following the line of a stream on your left. Cross a double stile and bear right to a waymarked post. Follow the arrow direction across the field to pass through a line of hawthorn trees. Bear right to a stile by the 'Manifold Valley Visitor Centre' notice.

37. Cross the stile and turn left back to the car park.

HIGH PEAK TRAIL – MONYASH

Hurdlow – High Peak Trail – Moscar Farm – Monyash – Limestone Way – Flagg – Pomeroy – High Peak Trail

MAP: O.S. Outdoor Leisure 24 The Peak District White Peak Area.

PARKING: Grid Ref. SK128659

DIRECTIONS: From the centre of Buxton take the A515 Ashbourne road. After 7 miles and having just passed *The Bull i' th' Thorn Hotel*, turn right signed Crowdecote/Longnor. In about 400 metres turn left into the Hurdlow High Peak Trail car park.

WALK DESCRIPTION:
An easy walk starting with a 2 mile and ending with a 1 mile pleasant walk along The High Peak Trail. Between these two sections you will follow field paths and tracks and part of the Limestone Way. You will visit Monyash, where *The Bull's Head* or a café offers a refreshment stop, and the outskirts of Flagg. Flagg Hall was once the home of the Fynney family descendants of Baron John Finnes warden of the Cinque Ports in 1086. Edward VIII is said to have ridden in the Flagg point-to-point races held every Easter Tuesday. *The Royal Oak* at the start of the walk, *The Duke of York* in Pomeroy and *The Bull i' the' Thorn* all offer refreshments.

ROUTE INSTRUCTIONS:
1. With your back to the buildings, bridge and gate, leave the car park to walk in a southerly direction down the High Peak Trail, passing the picnic tables.
2. After nearly two miles and before Parsley Hay turn left off the Trail by the High Peak notice board. Cross the stile.
3. Walk up the field to cross a stile then follow the wall on your left. Go through a gate and bear right to cross another stile. Cross a farm drive and keep straight on passing Moscar Farm then bear left to follow the wall on your left. Cross the stile in the field corner.
4. Turn left along the A515 for about 50 metres then cross the busy road and down a bank to go over a stile by the footpath post.
5. Bear slightly left aiming for the lower of two large trees by the wall ahead. Cross a squeeze stile under the tree. Bear right diagonally

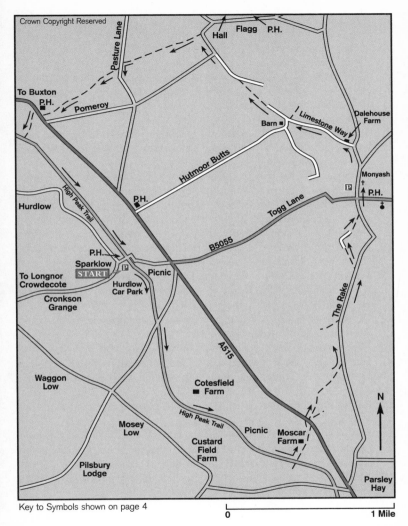

Key to Symbols shown on page 4

0   1 Mile

across the field corner to cross a waymarked stile. Walk almost diagonally across the next long field crossing a line of rough pitted ground. Cross the wall stile or gap below the field corner.

6. Bear left across the next field corner to cross a stile then bear right to walk towards and over a wooden stile. Bear right again to the road.

7. Turn left to follow the road for about ¾ mile. Just past a small copse of trees up on your left, turn left to go through the second of two farm gates. Bear very slightly right uphill to go through a very small gate by the farm gate.

8. Bear right to pass under power lines and through a small area of rock outcrops. Cross the stile and bear left down the field to cross the stile in the field corner. Turn right to go through a squeeze stile by the farm gate.

9. Follow a walled track for about ¼ mile down towards Monyash. The track bends right, is crossed by an old gate and stile and becomes very overgrown with a narrow path through it.

10. At the end of the track keep straight on to cross a stile by a gate. Walk down to the road and turn left into Monyash.

11. Cross the B5055. Walk down Chapel Street passing the small car park and the Methodist Chapel. At the road junction keep straight on following the Flagg/Taddington road. After nearly ½ mile from the B5055 crossroads, turn left at the Limestone Way footpath post by the converted barns.

12. Walk up the walled track passing Dalehouse Farm. After nearly half a mile keep straight on following a wall on your right to pass a stile on your right and a stone barn on your left.

13. Continue ahead to follow a path down an overgrown walled track. After about 250 metres cross a stile.

14. Bear right diagonally across the field to cross a wall stile above the field corner. Walk towards a small copse to cross the stile by the footpath post. Keep straight on following the wall on your left to join a farm drive.

15. Follow the farm drive down to the road, crossing one cattle grid via a stile.

16. Keep straight on along the road towards Flagg. Where the road bends sharp right into the village keep straight on to go through the gate ahead passing a gate on your left.

17. Turn left and follow the wall on your left up three fairly large fields and crossing three stiles.

18. Turn left up Pasture Lane for a few metres then turn right over the stile.

19. Follow the wall on your right up to a small stand of trees. Go through the gate ahead, across an enclosure and through the left-hand gate into the field.

20. Bear left up the field, cross two wall stiles and keep straight on up the middle of the next field to cross another wall stile. Bear right aiming

for a building to the right of a wood and a wall corner.

21. Just past the wall corner go over a stile (this area may be fenced off temporarily with a stile). Walk up the field, veering away from the wall on your right, to cross a stile by the field corner.

22. Turn right for a few metres to cross the road by *The Duke of York*. Cross a stile and walk across the yard by the Pomeroy Nursery. Go through the gate.

23. Follow the wall on your right which shortly bends round to the left. Pass the bridge over the Trail and turn right down the bank to cross the stile onto the High Peak Trail.

24. Turn left to follow the Trail for about 1 mile back to the car park.

WALK 13 - LONGSHAW ESTATE, Nr. HATHERSAGE   6½ MILES

UPPER BURBAGE BRIDGE - HIGGER TOR

Houndkirk Road – Burbage Rocks – Upper Burbage Bridge – Higger Tor – Millstone Edge – Surprise View car park – Burbage Brook – Longshaw Estate

MAP: Outdoor Leisure 1 The Peak District Dark Peak Area.

PARKING: Grid Ref. SK266801

DIRECTIONS: From Hathersage take the A6187 Sheffield road. After nearly 3 miles and having passed Surprise View car park and the B6521, then at *The Fox House Inn* bear right onto the Chesterfield road. In about 100 metres turn right into the Longshaw Estate car park.

WALK DESCRIPTION:
On a fine sunny day this is a very rewarding walk across open moorland with wonderful views up towards Stanage Edge and across the Derwent Valley. The return path follows the lovely Burbage Brook before entering the open woodland of Longshaw Estate. Higger Tor is a well-known rock-climbing venue and Carl Wark was once a hill fort thought to date back to the Dark Ages. There are many picnic sites along the route also refreshment stops at *The Fox House Inn* and the *National Trust Café* on the Longshaw Estate.

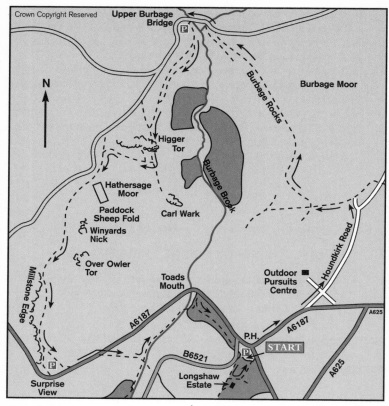

Crown Copyright Reserved

Upper Burbage Bridge

Burbage Moor

Burbage Rocks

N

Higger Tor

Burbage Brook

Hathersage Moor

Paddock Sheep Fold

Winyards Nick

Carl Wark

Over Owler Tor

Millstone Edge

Houndkirk Road

Toads Mouth

Outdoor Pursuits Centre

A6187

P.H.

A6187

A625

START

B6521

A625

Surprise View

Longshaw Estate

Key to Symbols shown on page 4

0   1 Mile

ROUTE INSTRUCTIONS:

1. Leave the car park via the main entrance and turn left back down the road to *The Fox House Inn*. Turn right to follow the A road to Sheffield for about ¼ mile then turn left onto a stoney track, Houndkirk Road.

2. Follow this track for ¾ mile passing through one gate. At the gas pipeline signs leave Houndkirk Road to walk along another track on your left; this narrows and bends round to the right before reaching another path where you turn left.

3. Follow the well-used moorland path for nearly ¼ mile to a waymarked post. Turn right to follow the rocky path across Burbage Rocks for just over 1 mile.

4. Cross the fence stile onto the lay-by and turn left down the road crossing the two bridges over Burbage Brook. Turn left to walk into the car park then turn right over the stile back onto the moors.

5. Take the right-hand fork to follow the path uphill. At the next fork of paths take either one as they join up after a few metres. As you approach Higger Tor, you will see the stepped path that you follow.

6. On reaching another path at a T-junction below the rocks, turn left at the waymarked post. Keep straight on to the edge of the rock out-crop. There are a number of ways down – choose one most suitable to you, aiming for the wide sandy track between Higger Tor and Carl Wark.

7. Follow this track downhill for about 100 metres until you meet a clear wide path on your right. Follow this path which runs parallel to Higger Tor, ignoring another path on your right leading up to the rocks.

8. Just before the end of the rock outcrop, turn left down through the bracken and heather to join a wider grass path. Turn left. On reaching a walled paddock over on your left, keep straight on towards a group of trees on your right to pick up a wall on your right.

9. Follow the main moorland path below the rocks of Winyards Nick and Over Owler Tor. After nearly ½ mile the path bends right to climb steeply up to the 'Open Country' sign and a stile (do not cross it).

10. Turn left to follow a fence on your right for nearly ½ mile above Millstone Edge. On reaching a stile and the 'Open Country' sign on your right, turn left to follow a path down to and through Surprise View car park.

11. Cross the busy main road and turn left along the footpath for about 200 metres. Turn right by two stone gateposts to go down the bank and through a small gate.

12. Follow the sunken path down to Burbage Brook. Turn left along the brookside path for about ½ mile then cross the footbridge on your right.

13. Follow a stone path uphill and round a right-hand bend. At a T-junction of paths turn right to walk through open woodland. Go through a swing gate and continue in the same direction.

14. Go through a small gate and turn right down the road for a few metres then cross the road to go through the gateway into the grounds of Longshaw Estate. Follow the drive and just before the Café and Visitor Centre, (open daily in the summer), turn left, then right at the car park notice. Follow the path back to the car park.

LYME PARK – GRITSTONE TRAIL

Lyme Park – Gritstone Trail via Bowstonegate – Brink Farm –
Bakestonedale Moor – West Park Gate – Lyme Park

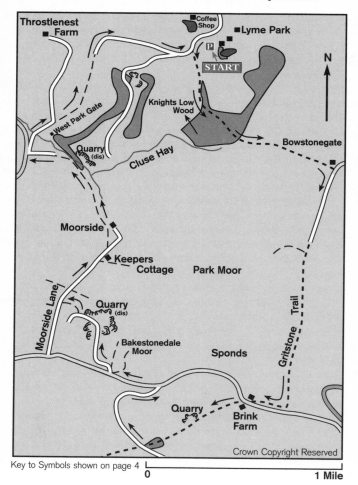

Key to Symbols shown on page 4

0   1 Mile

MAP: O.S. Outdoor Leisure 24 and 1 Peak District White Peak and Dark Peak.

PARKING: £3.50 for non-National Trust members. Grid Ref. SJ963823.

DIRECTIONS: From Buxton take the A5004 Whaley Bridge road. After 7 miles join the A6 and turn left to drive through Furness Vale, Newtown and into the outskirts of Disley. About ½ mile past the railway station take a very sharp left-hand turn into Lyme Park; it is signed with the brown National Trust sign. Drive through the park to the car park. Distance from Buxton to the car park is about 13 miles.

WALK DESCRIPTION:

Lyme Park is owned by the National Trust, is open from April to October and has much of interest. There is a coffee shop, a National Trust shop and extensive grounds for walks and picnics. The Gritstone Trail starts at the car park and runs for many miles south through Cheshire and Staffordshire. This walk follows the Trail for the first three miles where there are wonderful views. After leaving the Trail you follow field paths and tracks and cross through a disused quarry before entering Lyme Park back to the car park.

ROUTE INSTRUCTIONS:

1. From the car park continue along the park road with the lake to your right then, as you bend left, the lake is behind you. Ignore a park road up on your right and follow the Gritstone sign to go through a kissing gate.
2. Walk up the gravel track for about ¼ mile. Cross a ladder stile and keep straight on through the wood to cross another ladder stile.
3. Continue uphill, signed Bowstones, climbing the moorland for about ½ mile. Cross a ladder stile out of the National Trust area and walk up past the masts at Bowstones to cross a stile on your right (notice the ancient Saxon crosses in an enclosure).
4. Keep straight on to go through a small gate, still following the Gritstone Trail.
5. At first, the Trail is bounded by walls and fences. After the second stile keep straight on across open country. You will pass one waymarked sign and a 'footpath' post indicating a most interesting View Finder stone. Near the end of the trail cross two more stiles. The total distance from Bowstones to the road is about 1¼ miles.
6. Turn right along the road for about 325 metres to pass Brink Farm Cottage and Brink Farm. Turn left over a stile on your left by the footpath post and the Gritstone Trail sign.
7. Walk up the farm drive with the fence on your left. At a waymarked

post on your right bear off left up the bank of the track to another waymarked post at a wall corner, then bear slightly right down to a third waymarked sign to cross a stile.

8. Bear off left passing a small quarry up on your right and aiming for the start of a broken wall (the dry path through the reeds is not obvious). Cross the broken wall and turn left at the waymarked stone. Contour the hillside through the open stand of trees following the line of the broken wall down on your left (a good picnic area).

9. Cross a stile ahead of you then follow an unfenced track, leaving the Gritstone Trail. After about ½ mile, the track reaches the road. Turn left.

10. Follow the road for nearly ¼ mile. At the bottom of the hill turn right at the Bridleway sign to go up through a small gate and turn left up a moorland track, ignoring a narrower path straight ahead, and bending left then right up the wider track.

11. On reaching some gates go through the smaller gate and on up the moorland track passing a waymarked post. Keep straight on through the old quarry for a short way before turning left to go through another small gate. Continue on down a wide quarry track which bends right passing another waymarked post. At this point keep straight on up the quarry track (do not go round to the left). The track now descends. Go through a third small gate and join a stoney track. The distance covered through the quarry is nearly 400 metres.

12. Turn right and follow the track for about ¼ mile passing Keepers Cottage to cross a stile on your left signed 'Public Footpath to High Poynton'.

13. Keep straight on following a clear undulating path until you descend a small valley to cross a stream. Turn right up a rather muddy path to meet a wall on your right. Follow the wall to go through a gate in the field corner and keep straight on. Go down steep steps under the trees. Bear left away from the wall to go through a small metal gate.

14. Follow a track which soon joins another track coming in on the left. Keep straight along the track to pass Green Close Farm and Wayside Cottage before walking down to a minor road.

15. Turn sharp right by an old Methodist Chapel 1861 to follow the footpath sign along a tarmac track. Pass West Park Gate Farm then, where the track bends left, keep straight on up to cross a ladder stile by a gate.

16. Continue ahead up the grass track which shortly bends left. After about ½ mile go through a kissing gate back onto National Trust land.

17. Follow the wide stoney track round the hillside and at a T-junction turn left back to the car park.

RUSHUP EDGE – SPARROWPIT

**Mam Nick – Windy Knoll – Eldon Hill Quarries – Perry Dale –
Sparrowpit – A623 – Rushup Edge – Mam Nick**

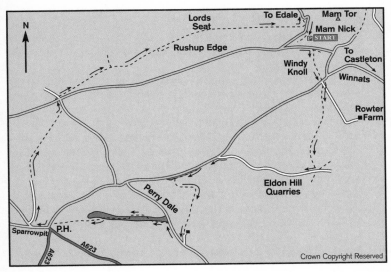

Key to Symbols shown on page 4

0   1 Mile

MAP: Outdoor Leisure 1 The Peak District Dark Peak Area.

PARKING: Grid Ref. SK123832

DIRECTIONS: From Castleton take the A6187. At the road fork take the
left-hand road to Speedwell Cavern. Follow the minor road up the
magnificent Winnats Pass. At the road junction turn right, then left after
about 400 metres. After just under ½ mile turn right into the Mam Nick pay
and display car park.

WALK DESCRIPTION:
A walk in the lesser-known area south of Rushup Edge. The route follows
wide grass paths and tracks before passing Eldon Hill quarries. The route
from Perry Dale to Sparrowpit follows little-used paths. *The Wanted Inn*

provides a half-way refreshment stop after which the route follows bridleways and well-used paths up onto Rushup Edge from where there are awe-inspiring views up to Kinder and the Edale Valley. Castleton with its many Blue John souvenir shops, cafés and restaurants and an information office is well worth a visit. The caves in the area are well signposted.

ROUTE INSTRUCTIONS:

1. Leave the car park and turn left back along the A625 for about 300 metres to turn right through a gate onto the National Trust Windy Knoll area.

2. Follow the wide grassy path bearing right at the disused quarry entrance and continue uphill to meet a wall on your right. Cross a stile by a gate.

3. Cross the road diagonally right to go through the gate signed 'Rowter Farm'. After about 20 metres leave the surfaced track and bear right across the field following a wide grass path and meeting a wall on your right. Cross a stile and keep straight on crossing two more stiles and keeping the wall on your right.

4. Cross a track to go over a wall stile by the gate then bear right to follow the stoney bridleway round Eldon Hill Quarries (quarry blasting 12.30 and 16.00 hours). After just over ¾ mile join the minor road and turn left.

5. Follow this road for about 250 metres then cross a ladder stile on your left and turn right to follow a rather overgrown path parallel to the road and below a quarry embankment, crossing one stile.

6. On reaching a track turn left. Where this track turns right keep straight on to cross a stile and then on down the hill. Cross a stile on your right by the footpath sign. This path may be overgrown.

7. Keep straight on along the bottom of the field to go through a gate then follow the wall on your right. At the wall corner bear right across the field corner to go through another gate. Now follow the wall on your left. Pass through a gate by the farm buildings and bear left down the field to the farm drive which you follow to the road.

8. Turn right up the Perry Dale road for about 400 metres to the start of a wood, cross the stile on your left. (There seems to be an informal path up the centre of the wood for nearly one mile, however the actual path is as described below).

9. Bear left round the end of the wall then climb steeply uphill keeping the wood on your right. Go through a wall gap ahead then almost immediately turn right through another gap to walk diagonally left

through the narrow wood and through another wall gap. Turn left on up the field; the wood is now on your left. You will meet a double wire fence; at this point cross a broken wall on your left. Now follow a wall on your right across the wood to cross a stile on your right. Keep straight on following the line of the old wall on your left. Cross two broken walls in the wood. Just past a right-hand bend in the wall cross a double stile on your left.

10. Turn right to follow the wall on your right. You may have to cross a stile over an electric fence. At the end of the wood cross the field towards a farm gate. Cross the stile. After a few metres bear left off the farm track.

11. Walk diagonally down across the field passing under the power lines and aiming for the left-hand end of a copse of trees and a barn. Cross the wall stile and bear right down the next field to cross a stile in the field corner.

12. Walk down to the road and turn left along the road for a few metres. Just before the road junction with the A623 and opposite *The Wanted Inn*, turn right. Walk down then up the minor road passing the Sparrowpit Methodist Church. At the first derestriction sign bear right. Follow the road uphill and round to the right then almost immediately turn right through a gate.

13. Follow a walled track which leads into a track with the wall only on the right before crossing a stile by a gate. Continue in the same direction for just over ¾ mile following a wall on your right and crossing five stiles.

14. Turn left up the minor road. At the T-junction cross the A625 to go over a stile by a gate. Turn right to follow a path parallel to the main road. After about 150 metres turn left.

15. Follow the well-used route up and across Rushup Edge for two miles. You will go through one gate and over five stiles ignoring all side turns and following the Castleton/Hope route.

16. At the end of the ridge the path drops steeply to near the road then turns left parallel to the road for a short way. Cross the stile onto the road and turn right up the road for about 100 metres. At the right-hand bend just past the gate up to Mam Tor, fork left onto a stone-stepped path which takes you back to the car park.

GLAPWELL – ROWTHORNE TRAIL

Rowthorne Trail – Longhedge Lane – Green Lane - Archaeological Way – Poulterwell Lane – Palterton – Glapwell

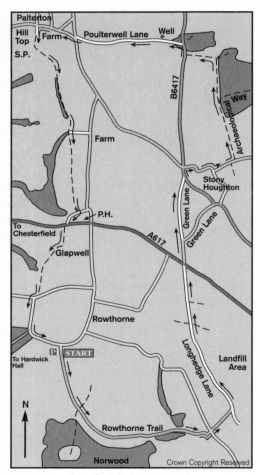

Key to Symbols shown on page 4

0   1 Mile

MAP: Explorer 269 Chesterfield and Alfreton.

PARKING:
Grid Ref. SK477646

DIRECTIONS:
From Alfreton take the A61 Chesterfield road. In the centre of Clay Cross turn right onto the A6175, following the one-way system and the M1 sign. Continue on the A6175 through North Wingfield and Williamthorpe. At the M1 junction take the last turn out of the island over the M1 onto the A617 Mansfield road. In nearly 1½ miles turn right at the crossroads in Glapwell signed Rowthorne. Follow this minor road for nearly 1 mile, passing through the hamlet of Rowthorne and ignoring all left and right turns. Turn left into the Derbyshire

County Council Rowthorne and Pleasley car park and picnic area.

WALK DESCRIPTION:
It is often thought that the best walks in Derbyshire are in the Peak District. Try this delightful easy route following tracks, bridleways and well-used waymarked paths across the undulating arable land east of Hardwick Hall. The long views and the high open aspect are reminiscent of East Anglia. It is a restful walk even though you are not far from the M1. It has the added advantage of no steep hills! Glapwell colliery was sunk in the 1880s and ceased production in 1974 since when the area has been landscaped as you will see along Longhedge Lane. The village pub *Young Vanish* was named after a famous 19th century racehorse. You can reach the pub by turning left along the A617 instead of right as instruction 20.

ROUTE INSTRUCTIONS:
1. From the car park walk back under the height entrance-beam and turn right to cross a stile onto the 'Trail'.
2. Follow the Rowthorne Trail for 1¼ miles until you reach the Derbyshire County Council Countryside Service and Rowthorne Trail notice on your left.
3. Turn right through a fence gap. At the surfaced lane, turn right uphill to cross a stile by a gate.
4. Turn left to follow a well-defined bridleway crossing the bridge over Batley Lane. After about 400 metres and at the top of a short slope, go through a swing gate and turn left.
5. Follow the bridleway for about 1¼ miles (Longhedge Lane) ignoring all side paths.
6. Cross the busy A617 to go down Green Lane. After 250 metres and where the road bends right, keep straight on along a wide track which shortly leads into a hedge- and tree-lined grassy bridleway.
7. Follow this bridleway for nearly ½ mile. On reaching the B6417 turn left for a few metres then turn right at the crossroads.
8. Follow this twisting restricted access road which after about 350 metres turns left signed 'Shirebrook 2'. After another 250 metres turn left at the electricity pylon.
9. Follow a wide track to cross a stile by a gate. Continue ahead following the Archaeological Way for nearly ½ mile and where it turns sharp right, <u>keep straight on.</u>
10. Follow the hedge and trees close on your right for nearly ¼ mile. At a T-junction of paths in a field corner turn left, still keeping the hedge close on your right. Pass through a squeeze stile.

11. Turn right up the road for about 250 metres then turn left at the Bridleway sign.

12. This track, known as Poulterwell Lane, first passes through a wood then becomes grassy and hedged. After just over ¾ mile cross the road.

13. Walk up Main Street into and through Palterton Village, ignoring all turnings off.

14. At the start of Rylah Hill and the decontrolled sign, turn left signed 'Glapwell 1½ m'.

15. Follow the track, passing Hill Top Farm, to cross a stile by a gate. In a few metres turn left following a farm track (this is a good picnic spot with extensive panoramic views).

16. Walk up to a waymarked post. Keep straight on, following the hawthorn bushes on your right and the open field on ypur left. Pass another waymarked post. At the footpath post follow the Glapwell route keeping the field boundary close on your right. Cross a stile by a gate.

17. Bear left then turn right in a few metres. Follow the field boundary close on your right. At the end of this very large field, cross a track and go up the bank.

18. Veer very slightly left to follow a path across the middle of the field aiming for a long barn two fields away. Pass through a hedge gap and continue in the same direction across the middle of the next field.

19. Cross a fence stile and keep straight on passing the end of the barn on your left. Cross a stile to walk down a surfaced path between the houses.

20. Turn left to walk down to the T-junction then turn right. Walk up to the main A617 road and cross it. Turn right for a few metres then turn left up steps by the footpath sign.

21. Follow the surfaced path to join Beech Crescent. Keep straight on for about 200 metres then turn right at the footpath sign to follow a surfaced path.

22. At the end of the path turn left down to the field. Bear slightly left across the field aiming for a wide gap in the hedge ahead of you. Go through the gap and continue ahead up the next field, passing under power lines then passing a line of six trees, at right angles to the field path, on your right. Continue uphill towards a power line pole. Cross the stile onto the minor road.

23. Turn right up Ault Hucknall Lane and in a few metres turn left. Follow the minor road which turns left after just under ¼ mile. After another 200 metres turn right to go through a small gateway.

24. Follow the woodland path back to the car park.

MONSAL DALE – ASHFORD-IN-THE-WATER

White Lodge car park on th A6– Monsal Dale – Monsal Head – Monsal Trail – Ashford-in-the-Water – Great Shacklow Wood

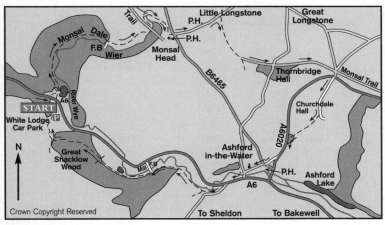

Key to Symbols shown on page 4

0 _____ 1 Mile

MAP: O.S. Outdoor Leisure 24 The Peak District White Peak Area.

DIRECTIONS: From the island in the centre of Bakewell take the A6 Buxton road. After 3½ miles, and having passed the turn to Ashford on your right, turn left into the White Lodge pay and display car park. Grid Ref. SK171706.

WALK DESCRIPTION:
A varied and interesting walk, especially in the Spring, along Monsal Dale and Trail then on a less popular path down to the picturesque village of Ashford-in-the-Water. Here you will find a number of refreshment stops. Leaving the village via the pretty packhorse bridge and a very short stretch of the A6, the return route is along the shaded undulating path through Great Shacklow Wood which is a riot of colour in May.

ROUTE INSTRUCTIONS:
1. From the car park, walk past the pay and display machine on your left

to go down three steps. Cross the busy A6 to go through a wall gap and down five steps.

2. Follow the well-defined path down the field to cross stepping stones and a stile. Continue along the wide lower riverside path signed Monsal Dale. Ignore all side paths. Eventually you will pass a footbridge and the weir on your right.

3. After about 1 mile and on approaching the viaduct pass through a squeeze stile by a gate and walk under the viaduct to continue along the riverside path. In about 250 metres turn right to cross the footbridge over the River Wye.

4. Walk up past the farm and turn right signed 'Bridle Way Monsal Head'. Follow the rather steep path for just under ¼ mile up to Monsal Head ignoring all side paths.

5. At the top go through the larger of the two wall gaps and walk up to the *Monsal View Café*. Walk past the *Monsal View Café* and the hotel to cross the B6465. Walk down the road into Little Longstone. After passing the *Pack Horse Inn* and opposite a farm entrance on your left, turn right to go through a small gate signed 'Ashford and Monsal Trail'.

6. Keep straight on across two fields and through two gates then follow the path and wall up the third field to cross a stile on your right.

7. Turn left along the trail for just over ¾ mile. You will pass under three bridges and pass Thornbridge Hall and the old station. Immediately after crossing over a road bridge turn left down a path to the road.

8. Turn left down to the T-junction then walk under the bridge to follow the Ashford/Baslow road. In a few metres at the next road junction, follow the Ashford sign round the grass triangle to cross the A6020. Walk up the minor road signed 'Private No Parking' and 'Public Footpath'.

9. Follow this road for nearly ½ mile passing Churchdale Lodge and at the entrance to Churchdale Hall bear left to cross a ladder stile by a gate. A few metres further on leave the drive to cross a stile on the right by a metal gate.

10. Keep straight on following the boundary wall of Churchdale Hall on your right and the ha-ha wall in front of the hall. Cross the stile by a stand of trees. Bear very slightly left across the middle of the field to cross a fence stile. Continue in the same direction to cross another fence stile. Follow a path downhill through the trees to go through a small gate and across a stream then on up to go through a squeeze stile.

11. Turn left along the A6020 (it is advisable to use the pavement on the

right-hand side of the road). As you approach Ashford stay on the pavement leaving the A6020. At the road junction turn right into the village.

12. Walk past *The Devonshire Arms* on your left, following the road as it bends round to the left into Church Street. Pass *The Bulls Head Inn* and the church on your right. Walk up to the octagonal shelter built to commemorate the Queen's Silver Jubilee 1952-1977. Cross the packhorse bridge over the beautiful River Wye.

13. Turn right down the A6 for about 250 metres. Turn left along the minor road to Sheldon. After about 325 metres, and where the road starts to climb and bend left, bear right off the road down a short track to go through a small gate.

14. Follow the riverside path for just over ½ mile crossing two stiles and ignoring all side paths. On reaching a small bridge and old mill buildings, turn left to walk up behind the buildings. Now follow the pretty undulating winding path through Great Shacklow Wood for nearly one mile. Ignore all side paths.

15. Cross a stile and bear right descending the stoney path out of the wood. Continue on down the meandering shale path. Pass the sign to Deep Dale on your left. Follow the Bridleway sign to A6 and White Lodge. Cross a stile and turn right down the rocky path.

16. Pass a waymarked post on your left and follow the clearly-defined path, crossing two stiles, back to the car park.

TADDINGTON – DEEP DALE

White Lodge car park on the A6 – Taddington Field – Taddington – Flagg – Johnson Lane – Deep Dale

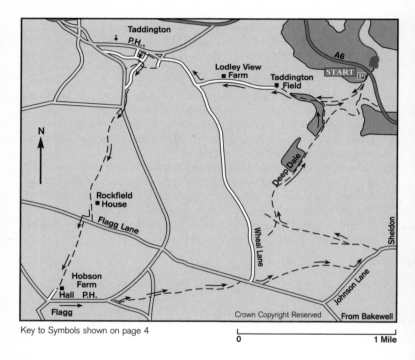

Key to Symbols shown on page 4

0　　　　　　　　　　　　　　　　　　　　1 Mile

MAP: O.S. Outdoor Leisure 24 The Peak District White Peak Area.

DIRECTIONS: From the island in the centre of Bakewell take the A6 Buxton road. After 3½ miles, and having passed the turn to Ashford on your right, turn left into the White Lodge pay and display car park. Grid Ref. SK171706.

WALK DESCRIPTION:

This walk has wonderful views across the undulating countryside of mid-Derbyshire. The route follows little-used field and dale paths and country lanes away from the more populated parts of the Peak District. There is one steep descent and one steep ascent into and out of Deep Dale. *The Queen's Arms Inn* in Taddington is a suitable refreshment stop. Taddington is one of the highest villages in England being 1,000ft above sea level.

ROUTE INSTRUCTIONS:

1. Leave the car park by walking up past the picnic tables. Cross a stile and follow a well-defined path, with the road down on your left, to cross another stile. In a few yards, at a waymarked post up on your right, turn right.
2. Follow a less well-defined path uphill, climb a low limestone outcrop and continue ahead with a fence then a gully down on your left. Cross the stile ahead. In about 100 metres turn left over and through a squeeze stile which may be somewhat hidden under the foliage.
3. Turn right up the dale, following a wall on your right for about 250 metres after which the dale opens out and is less rocky.
4. Near the top of the dale pass through a squeeze stile or the wall gap. Walk up the rough narrow field to cross a wall stile by the footpath post then bear right up the next field to go through a small gate below Taddington Field.
5. Turn left to follow the farm road for about ½ mile, passing Lodley View Farm.
6. At the T-junction turn right. Follow the minor road for about ½ mile.
7. On reaching Taddington keep straight on up through the village to join a road coming in on the right. Continue ahead, passing the chapel, to *The Queen's Arms Inn*.
8. Turn left opposite the Inn and walk up the lane, passing a garage on your left. By a gate continue on up a narrow walled track until you reach the steps. Turn left along a walled track for about 100 metres to a footpath sign and T-junction.
9. Turn right up a wide sunken track for about 325 metres to join the road.
10. Turn left for about 200 metres passing a lane on your right then immediately cross a stile on your right.
11. Follow the waymarked footpath sign diagonally across the field to go through the left-hand wall gap and keep straight on in the same direction round a small hill. Cross the stile in the middle of the opposite wall. Keep straight on to cross the line of an old wall then on to cross the stile ahead.
12. Keep straight on across the next field to go through a gateway then

bear right across the field corner to go through another gateway. Keep straight on passing a field mound on your left then descend the field to cross a squeeze stile by a gate.

13. Bear left diagonally across the next field. Cross the stile and turn left down the long narrow field to cross the stile.

14. Turn right along the road for about 50 metres then turn left at the footpath sign to cross the stile.

15. Keep straight on across the large field passing a single ash tree on your right. Go through a squeeze stile just below a wall corner.

16. Follow the narrow path through an area of scrub and low trees and crossing two wooden stiles.

17. Keep straight on towards farm buildings. If the field is fenced off turn left then right following a farm track. Cross a stile by a gate and then a ladder stile if the electric fence across the yard is in use. Walk through the farmyard and then on down the drive to the road in Flagg.

18. Turn left to follow the Monyash/Taddington road through the village passing *The Plough Inn* on your left (not always open at lunchtime). In just under ½ mile turn right signed Monyash. In about 100 metres and hidden under a larch tree, cross a small wall stile on your left.

19. Keep straight on following the wall on your left to pass through a wall gap and continue uphill to go through a squeeze stile. Bear right towards the wall on your right. Cross the wall stile near the field corner. Keep straight on down the field.

20. Cross two stiles and the road in-between.

21. Walk up the field to the wall corner then follow the wall on your right. Cross the stile in the field corner and keep straight on aiming for the power line pole in the opposite wall. Cross the wall stile and keep straight on to cross another stile.

22. Bear slightly left up the next field to walk below the stoney outcrops and cross a farm track to go over a wall stile. Turn left to follow the wall on your left and then over a stile on your left. Bear right across the field to go through a squeeze stile in the field corner.

23. Turn right to walk down the road towards Sheldon for about 200 metres. Turn left over a gated stile by a short footpath post.

24. Bear right and continue in more or less the same north-easterly direction crossing six fields, five stiles and one gate. In the fourth field keep the power lines on your left and in the sixth field bear left to the field corner.

25. Turn left up the road for about 300 metres then turn left over a wall stile by the footpath post.

26. Bear very slightly left down the field to cross a squeeze stile just above